Hua-yen Buddhism

Titles in the IASWR Series

Hua-yen Buddhism

The Jewel Net of Indra

Francis H. Cook

The Pennsylvania State University Press
University Park and London

Published in cooperation with
The Institute for Advanced Studies of World Religions
New York, N.Y.

Library of Congress Cataloging in Publication Data
Cook, Francis H
  Hua-yen Buddhism.

  Includes bibliographical references and index.
  1. Kegon (Sect)—Doctrines. 2. Avataṃsakasūtra—
Criticism, interpretation, etc. I. Title.
BQ8218.C66   294.3'92   76-43288
ISBN 0-271-02190-X

Dedicated in memory of my father,
Harold M. Cook

Contents

Preface

This book about the world view of a Chinese form of Buddhism called Hua-yen (Flower Ornament) is the result of about a decade of serious, uninterrupted study of the various forms which Buddhist thought and practice have taken since their origins in India in the fifth century B.C. During the six years when I was a graduate student in the Program in Buddhist Studies at the University of Wisconsin, I became increasingly attracted to this important and hitherto neglected system of Buddhist thought. As scholars do, I staked out the territory in which I wished to do my future explorations, and for the past several years, I have devoted most of my time to the translation and close study of Hua-yen materials. I have come to admire Hua-yen philosophy greatly. It is out of this admiration for such a grand and satisfying world view, as well as the considerations below, that this book grows, in the hope that Hua-yen will prove to be equally interesting to both specialists in Asian religion and those nonspecialists who for one reason or another find the study of Buddhism to be a fruitful use of time. Keeping in mind the mixed nature of readers of books of this sort, I have tried to be as thorough and accurate as such a study demands without burdening the nonspecialist with a heavy freight of scholarly apparatus. For specialists, I have used notes wherever necessary and placed them in the back of the book. On the assumption that the subject is itself both interesting and convincing, I have avoided the temptation to overinflate the language with professional or intellectual jargon in an attempt to further elevate the subject.

There are several reasons why I decided to write this book. First, as already indicated, Hua-yen Buddhism is a fascinating and intrinsically interesting subject. Although it may be the deluded fancy of a person who has spent too many nights pondering over the meaning of seventh-century Chinese Buddhist texts, I would like to believe that the picture of existence described in Hua-yen literature is truly beautiful, grand, and inspiring. What is more, we are assured by wise men of the Hua-yen tradition that we do in fact dwell in such a universe constantly, though we are hardly aware of it. For the reader with a working knowledge of Western philosophy, religion, art, and science, the Hua-yen world will prove to be not only new and different, but challenging, and not at all self-evident. The reader is going to have to perform the very difficult task of opening his or her mind and making it flexible. But the rewards of this effort will be a new understanding of a view of existence which is exciting in its possibilities. Even the reader who can appreciate only slightly such a view of things will have taken the first step of that journey which Hua-yen texts refer to as "entering the *dharma-dhātu*." To the reader whose mind is forever made up that reality lies in tables of statistics showing the proportion of third-generation Irish in Boston who own television sets, the Hua-yen description of the true nature of things is going to seem to be sheer nonsense. He is going to laugh, but to paraphrase Lao-tzu, if he didn't laugh it would not be worth serious consideration.

Another reason for writing this book is that I hope that it will add something to our knowledge of what Chinese Buddhism was, and how it developed. Some excellent studies of pre-T'ang Chinese Buddhism have appeared in Japanese and Western languages in the past few decades, and some notable studies of T'ang culture in certain areas have now appeared also, but next to nothing has been written yet in the West on this form of Chinese Buddhism which has been acknowledged by Oriental religionists and students of Chinese culture to be the high-water mark of Buddhist philosophical effort. One consideration, then, is the obvious one of attempting to describe Hua-yen Buddhism carefully and accurately. At the same time, we need to know much more about *how* Hua-yen came to be what it is. What are its connections with parent Indian thought forms? How, if at all, is it related to indigenous Chinese systems of thought such as Taoism? While it is not my purpose to deal explicitly with the question of adaptation and assimilation, I hope that some light will be shed on them.

Finally, a third reason. I wonder if the Hua-yen world view can be seriously considered as an adequate, satisfying description of existence. Perhaps, again, it is the lamentable result of too many nights of coffee, pipe smoke, and small Chinese characters, but I have come to ask myself if the structure and nature of reality as shown by the Hua-yen masters is, after all, that remote and implausible, despite the vast gulf that separates our own time and place from T'ang period Chinese Buddhism. Western presuppositions have brought us to a world view vastly different from that of a Chinese Buddhist of the late seventh century. Moreover, the Hua-yen view of existence is a religious and ethical view, finally, and modern Western man, despite his pious protestations, has no real understanding of, or concern with, religious values anymore. But, with regard to the former problem, are we not just as separated from the worlds of Plato, Jesus, Shakespeare, and Bach? The world of Jesus two thousand years ago on the eastern end of the Mediterranean sea (and really an Oriental world!) has practically nothing in common with Western culture of the twentieth century. If a man living in London were to discover the Hebrew-Christian Bible manuscript for the first time today (and hence we would not be heirs to that tradition), translate, and publish it, the world view as divulged by that old book would certainly appear to be as implausible, irrelevant, and perhaps silly as that given in Hua-yen books. In other words, the plausibility or cogency of an idea is not always necessarily intrinsic to the material, but often seems to come from familiarity. That Jesus, Plato, or Shakespeare, or even a nineteenth-century Romantic poet, can communicate with us over the distances in time and place is partly due to the unbroken tradition stretching from them down to us. Put in another way, they make sense to us, have meaning to us, because they have become part of what we are. Without that unbroken tradition, it is, it must be agreed, difficult to seriously confront an alien tradition.

But familiarity does not make an idea true. The only real test of an idea is the effect it has on our lives, the way it helps us to organize our experience in a satisfying manner, in the general manner in which it forcibly shapes our thought and conduct. If a man's thoughts can do this, they can transcend the centuries. The reader must, therefore, put aside his cultural prejudices and bigotries and ask himself seriously if the Hua-yen picture of existence is *ipso facto* false or incredible *simply* because it is the product of a race of people and a time so different from his own. This is difficult to do, but in the ability to journey courageously outside one's own intellectual and cultural parish lies the only hope for a true civilization.

Why, then, should Hua-yen not present its case along with that of all the other philosophies that vie for our attention? The poor Western citizen is confronted with a real clamor of competing voices; he is implored to accept Science (or "Scientism"), Marxism, Capitalism, Cartesianism, Atheistic Humanism, Behaviorist Psychology, Positivism, Neo-thomism, and Consumerism, as well as any one of several dozen new, modern varieties of Christianity. Often, we make a choice, frequently out of exhaustion, but oddly enough, when we choose, we always choose the close at hand, for we feel that there is something alien and irrelevant (and maybe unsafe) in a philosophy created by Orientals or someone else not more or less just like us. Lately, it is true, a few have turned to Zen or Tibetan Tantra, and a few have expressed admiration and respect for native American Indian beliefs, but these are still statistically rare. When a man gives his heart to some new philosophy, it is because his heart has been there all the time. There are few real converts. Thus, he turns to Marx, sensitivity training, or Billy Graham. They are familiar and the change is not radical. So, here is Hua-yen to offer its voice. At one time, such a suggestion would have been intellectually risky, but I am encouraged by certain developments in the last few decades, in the increasing interest in Whitehead's process philosophy and in the increasing willingness to consider the implications of Einstein's theory of relativity, both of which bear startling similarities to Hua-yen, in great part if not wholly, and in spirit if not in language and intent. These developments have helped in no small way to make such a book as this feasible.

The reader may be forewarned that Hua-yen thought is difficult to understand, and without a reasonably good grounding in the basics of Indian Buddhism, much of the richness and beauty of Hua-yen will be lost. I have tried to help by including one chapter on the most important Indian Buddhist ideas to have some effect on the formation of Hua-yen, but considerations of space preclude any more lengthy discussion. For the serious reader who wants to pursue Hua-yen as well armed as possible, I would recommend some of the excellent books on general Indian Buddhist ideas now in print.

Buddhism has had a long and extraordinarily rich history, spanning 2,500 years in time and half the globe we live on. From its birthplace in India, it has traveled steadily east to enrich the cultures of first China, then Japan. Now, it would seem that the movement has reached the troubled shores of America and Europe in the middle of the twentieth century, where serious groups of Western Buddhists have sprung up all over. The uninformed reader would undoubtedly be startled to learn just how many Buddhist groups there are now in Europe and the United States. We are still in the position of saying and believing absurd things about this religion, the impact of which we are just now beginning to feel to any extent. Part of the value which this book may have lies in the fact that almost all (but not all) these forms of Buddhism look to Hua-yen for their philosophical foundation. This is particularly true of Zen, which is now the most widely spread form practiced. While Zen and some other forms are "practical" in that the main emphasis is on *doing*, rather than believing, reading, etc., the very truth which is the goal of this practice is precisely the view of things taught in systematic fashion by Hua-yen. If we are to cease believing and saying the silly things we do about Buddhism, we will have to have a much better understanding not only of the things it does (i.e., meditation) but of its goal as well. One of the elements of this understanding is the Hua-yen description of the world as seen by the enlightened. If the reader can understand the Hua-yen vision of reality, he will be better able to understand not only the more profound experiences of his Chinese and Japanese brothers, but also of those closer Western brothers of his who have given their hearts and minds to Buddhism. Perhaps this is as good a reason as any for the following pages.

The primary source for this book is a treatise called, in Chinese, *Hua-yen i-ch'eng chiao i fen-ch'i chang*. In the pages that follow, I will refer to it as the "Treatise." It was composed by Fa-tsang, the third patriarch of the Hua-yen school, at the end of the seventh century. Although there are several versions of this text, I have chosen that of the *Taishō Shinshū Daizōkyō*, which is the Japanese edition of the Chinese collection of Buddhist literature. It is an excellent text and any deviations from other versions which it shows are minor and inconsequential. This text is number 1866, in volume 45 of the *Taishō* edition, occupying pages 477–509. Wherever I have quoted from this text, I have indicated the source by showing the page and register within square brackets, thus [502b], and such references are always only to the Treatise. Other sources will be cited in the notes.

I have also relied heavily on three of the most useful commentaries on Fa-tsang's Treatise for my own reading and interpretation of the text.

1. *Kegon go kyō shō shiji ki*, in three volumes, composed during the Nara period in Japan. It is the oldest of the commentaries in either Chinese or Japanese. The text exists in the *Taishō Shinshū Daizōkyō*, in volume 72, *Dai Nippon Bukkyō Zensho*, volume 10, and *Bukkyō Taikei*, volumes 13 and 14.

2. *Tsūro-ki*, by the Japanese monk Gyōnen. Only 39 of the original 72 volumes are extant. Texts are in the *Taishō*, volume 72, *Dai Nippon Bukkyō Zensho*, volumes 9 and 10, and in *Bukkyō Taikei*, volumes 13 and 14.

3. *Wu chiao chang fu ku chi*, a Sung Dynasty commentary by Shih-hui. Texts exist in the *Manji Zokuzōkyō*, 2.8.3, and in the *Bukkyō Taikei*, volume 14.

I am indebted as well to the work of numerous Japanese scholars, for whom Hua-yen Buddhism is as familiar as, say, Methodism is for many in the United States. Their work, on historical and doctrinal matters, is indispensable to the study of Hua-yen. Wherever such a debt exists, I have so indicated.

My debts are, as a matter of fact, almost as extensive as the interrelationships described in the Hua-yen treatises. Professor Minoru Kiyota, my friend and teacher, first made me aware of the importance and value of Hua-yen thought, and had he not encouraged me to look into it, as well as to learn the Japanese necessary for its study, there would be one fewer book on Buddhism. Professor Richard Robinson was a very severe critic, constantly asking those embarrassing questions which made me return to the Chinese again and again. His insistence always on accurate readings of primary source materials made success possible.

His death in 1970 was a terrible loss for Buddhist Studies, as well as a personal loss. A generous Fulbright Fellowship for study in Japan from 1966 to 1968 made it possible for me to acquire many hard-to-get materials, to have a year and a half of luxurious time in which to do nothing but study Hua-yen literature, and to meet and talk with authoritative Japanese experts. Among the latter, I am especially grateful for the friendly help and support of Professors Makita, Nagao Gadjin, and Kajiyama Yuichi, of Kyoto University, and my friend and fellow researcher Aramaki Noritoshi of the Institute for Humanistic Studies, Kyoto University. The memory of many fruitful and pleasant hours in their company is one of the few treasures I am greedy enough to hang on to. Finally, my wife Betty contributed immeasurably to my being able to pursue Buddhist Studies while in graduate school and in Japan. Though her help took many forms, it would have been invaluable if for no other reason than that she has always supported me in my belief that the study of Buddhism is worthwhile. My debts extend beyond these, also, but where do they end? May the help of all these earn them countless *kalpas* in the Tushita Heavens.

An earlier work, C.C. Chang's *Buddhist Teaching of Totality*, is the first full-length treatment of Hua-yen thought in a Western language, but I have several reservations about some of its interpretations. Yet it can be recommended for its sympathetic discussion of the general outlines of Hua-yen cosmology. The reader could do no better than to read it before taking up this book.

Francis H. Cook

University of California, Riverside
1975

I

The Jewel Net of Indra

Western man may be on the brink of an entirely new understanding of the nature of existence. The work of classification and analysis which was born from the work of ancient Greek civilization has borne its fruit in the overwhelming success of Western man in manipulating the natural world, including himself. This conquest and manipulation has proceeded without pause, each success engendering new possibilities and successes, and there is reason to believe that this manipulation and exploitation will continue. However, some have begun to wonder if we have not had too much success; the very virtuosity with which we manipulate the natural world has brought us, according to some critics, to the thin line separating success from terrible disaster. Only very recently has the word "ecology" begun to appear in our discussion, reflecting the arising of a remarkable new consciousness of how all things live in interdependence. The traditional methods of analysis, classification, and isolation tended to erect boundaries around things, setting them apart in groups and thereby making easier their manipulation, whether intellectually or technologically. The ecological approach tends rather to stress the interrelatedness of these same things. While not naively obliterating distinctions of property and function, it still views existence as a vast web of interdependencies in which if one strand is disturbed, the whole web is shaken. The ecological viewpoint has not, that is, brought into question the ancient distinctions of property and function which lie behind a brilliant technology. Honey bees and apple blossoms remain what they have always been in our eyes, but added to this way of knowing is another, newer way—the knowledge that these entities need each other for survival itself. This understanding comes to us in the nature of a revelation; an eternally abiding truth has burst upon our consciousness, with an urgent message concerning our life. This new knowledge demands, in fact, a complete reassessment of the manner in which things exist. Perhaps this revelation is not yet closed, and in time we may come to perceive that this interdependency is not simply biological and economic, a matter of bees and blossoms, or plankton and oxygen, but a vastly more pervasive and complicated interdependency than we have so far imagined.

But this book is not about ecology, at least not directly, and not at all in the sense in which we now use the word. It presents a view of man, nature, and their relationship which might be called ecological in the more pervasive and complicated sense mentioned above, one which we might, in fact, call "cosmic ecology." It is a Buddhist system of philosophy which first appeared in a written, systematic form in China in the seventh century, and it was the characteristic teaching of what came to be known as the Hua-yen school of Buddhism. It is a view of existence which is for the most part alien to Western ways of looking at things, but it is a world view well worth consideration, not only as a beautiful artifact appealing to the esthetic sense, but perhaps as a viable basis for conduct, no less plausible than the traditional Western basis.

We may begin with an image which has always been the favorite Hua-yen method of exemplifying the manner in which things exist. Far away in the heavenly abode of the great god Indra, there is a wonderful net which has been hung by some cunning artificer in such a manner that it stretches out infinitely in all directions. In accordance with the extravagant tastes of deities, the artificer has hung a single glittering jewel in each "eye" of the net, and since the net itself is infinite in dimension, the jewels are infinite in number. There hang the jewels, glittering like stars of the first magnitude, a wonderful sight to behold. If we now arbitrarily select one of these jewels for inspection and look closely at it, we will discover that in its polished surface there are reflected *all* the other jewels in the net, infinite in number. Not only that, but each of the jewels reflected in this one jewel is also reflecting all the other jewels, so that there is an infinite reflecting process occurring. The Hua-yen school has been fond of this image, mentioned many times in its literature, because it symbolizes a cosmos in which there is an infinitely repeated interrelationship among all the members of the cosmos. This relationship is said to be one of simultaneous *mutual identity* and *mutual intercausality*.

If we take ten coins as symbolizing the totality of existence and examine the relationship existing among them, then, according to Hua-yen teaching, coin one will be seen as being identical with the other nine coins. Simultaneously, coin two will be seen as being identical with the other nine coins, and so on throughout the collection of coins. Thus, despite the fact that the coins may be of different denominations, ages, metals, and so on, they are said to be completely identical. This is said to be the *static* relationship of the coins. If we take these same ten coins again and examine their *dynamic* relationship, then, according to the Hua-yen masters, they will be seen as being totally interdependent or intercausal (depending on point of view). Seen in this way, coin one is said to be the cause for the totality of coins which are considered as being dependent on the first coin for their being. Coin one, that is, is the support, while the total group is that which is supported. Since that particular totality could not exist without the support of coin one, that coin is said to be the sole cause for the totality. However, if we shift our attention to coin two and now examine its relationship to the other nine coins, the same can now be said of this coin. It is the sole cause for the existence of the totality of ten coins. From the standpoint of *each* of the ten coins, it can be said that that coin is the sole cause for the whole. However, the cause-result relationship is even more fluid than this, for while each coin can, from the stand-point of the one coin, be said to act as sole cause for the whole, simultaneously the whole acts as cause for the one coin in question, for the coin only exists and has any function at all within the total environment. It can never be a question of the coin existing outside its environment, because since the ten coins symbolize the totality of being, a coin outside the context of the ten coins would be a nonentity. Thus each individual is at once the cause for the whole and is caused by the whole, and what is called existence is a vast body made up of an infinity of individuals all sustaining each other and defining each other. The cosmos is, in short, a self-creating, self-maintaining, and self-defining organism. Hua-yen calls such a universe the *dharma-dhātu*, which we may translate as "cosmos" or "universe" if we wish, with the proviso that it is not the universe as commonly imagined, but rather the Hua-yen universe of identity and interdependence.

Such a universe is not at all familiar to Western people. The Judeo-Christian religious tradition and the Greek philosophical tradition have bequeathed to their posterity a view of existence very much different from that conceived by the Chinese. It differs in several respects. First, it has been, and to some extent still is, a universe which must be explained in terms of a divine plan, with respect to both its beginning and its end. The Hua-yen world is completely nonteleological. There is no theory of a beginning time, no concept of a creator, no question of the purpose of it all. The universe is taken as a given, a vast fact which can be explained only in terms of its own inner dynamism, which is not at all unlike the view of twentieth-century physics. Moreover, our familiar world is one in which relationships are rather limited and special. We have blood relationships, marital relationships, relationships with a genus or species, relationships in terms of animate and inanimate, and the like, but it is hard for us to imagine how anything is related to everything else. How am I related to a star in Orion? How am I even related to an Eskimo in Alaska, except through the tenuous and really nonopera-tive relationship of species? I certainly don't feel related to these other things. In short, we find it much easier to think in terms of isolated *beings*, rather than one

Being. Being is just that, a unity of existence in which numerically separate entities are all interrelated in a profound manner. Beings are thought of as autonomous, isolated within their own skins, each independent by and large from all the rest of the beings (both animate and inanimate). The "mystic" who speaks of identity with such things as animals, plants, and inanimate objects, as well as other men, is an object of ridicule. The Hua-yen universe is essentially a universe of identity and total intercausality; what affects one item in the vast inventory of the cosmos affects every other individual therein, whether it is death, enlightenment, or sin. Finally, the Western view of existence is one of strict hierarchy, traditionally one in which the creator-god occupies the top rung in the ladder of being, man occupies the middle space, and other animals, plants, rocks, etc., occupy the bottom. Even with the steady erosion of religious interest in the West, where the top rung of the ladder has for many become empty, there still exists the tacit assumption that man is the measure of all things, that this is his universe, that somehow the incalculable history of the vast universe is essentially a human history. The Hua-yen universe, on the other hand, has no hierarchy. There is no center, or, perhaps if there is one, it is everywhere. Man certainly is not the center, nor is some god.

It must be admitted that the traditional anthropocentric universe has begun to fade under the careful scrutiny of people who are not sentimentalists or who do not childishly seek security in baseless assumptions. A physicist, or a philosopher such as Whitehead, would have to admit that comfortable old concepts such as the distinction of subject and object, or that of agent and act, metaphysical entities such as souls and selves, or even more fundamental notions such as the absoluteness of time and space, are untenable in the light of objective and serious inquiry. The Western world is alive with new ideas, but so far these ideas have not trickled down to the mass consciousness. Most people still have a deep faith in solid substances and believe that their feelings, ideas, and even their own bodies belong to, or inhere in, some mysterious but seemingly irrefutable substance called a self.

It has been said that you cannot kill an idea, but it is even more difficult to see a new idea get a hearing in the community of men. Shrinking from a reality which he assumes will demean him, man hangs on to his old habits of thought, which are really prejudices, just as he clung to his security blanket in his crib. The anthropocentric bias, particularly, has appeared in one form or another down through Western history. It is of course endemic in the Hebraic and Christian traditions, and it has also given rise to dreadful philosophy for a period of hundreds of years—in Cartesianism, with its affirmation of human consciousness and its view of dead nature, in the "Great Chain of Being" of the eighteenth-century philosophers, and even today among the positivists, in whom we detect a positivism which shrinks from taking the ultimate step in its positivism. The most ingenious attempts of Western thinkers to erect a satisfying picture of existence has resulted, in short, in a not too surprising conclusion that while he is less than a god, he stands just below the angels, superior to and apart from all other things. One may ask whether this conclusion has not risen out of a pathetic self-deception.

It is a truism that a culture reveals its fundamental assumptions and presuppositions in its art forms, and it is partly for this reason that the study of art is so rewarding. In European art, at least up to the advent of the Romantic movement, a representative, and perhaps dominant, genre has been the portrait. To walk through the rooms of a large art museum is to receive an eloquent testimonial concerning the preoccupation of Western man for the last several hundred years. If we examine one of these paintings, we find that it will be dominated by a face or several faces. The artist has drawn upon every resource of his genius and materials to render the face realistic, lifelike. It is invariably grave and composed, befitting a person who had no doubts as to his worth in the general scheme of things. Are ye not of more worth than many sparrows? Yes, of course! Every quirk of personality is here, along with the warts, bumps, hollows, and spidery lines of much frowning and laughing. The clothes, too, are lovingly painted; we have, in gazing at the portrait, an almost tactile sense of the stiffness and roughness of lace, the suave, warm plushness of velvet, and rich, hard luxury of silk. Rings, brooches, and pendants garnish the figure, glinting weightily with gold and silver. The skillful use of chiaroscuro bestows on the figure the roundness and solidity of life. But there is something else too, though we are in danger of overlooking it in our justified concentration on the grand face and figure dominating the canvas. Over the shoulder of the subject we detect a tiny fragment of world, perhaps seen through the tiny window of the lord's palace. If we do not look sharply, it may not even register on our consciousness, but in its own way, it is an important part of the picture for it tells us much. It occupies, in some paintings, only a hundredth part of the whole canvas, or, if it fills in the background, the coloring and style are such that the scene serves only as an unobtrusive backdrop for the real focal point of the picture. It is there for several reasons; it helps the painter avoid a dull and unimaginative background for the human foreground; it often contains symbols which help us "read" the meaning of the painting; or it defines and places in its correct context (seventeenth-century Florence, the world, etc.) the true subject. However, all these uses of the natural world add up to one; it serves as a backdrop for the human drama, which is not only what painting is about but what the universe is all about. Man still dwells comfortably in the pre-Copernican universe, where the world is a stage created for the most important of dramas, the human one. Even in the nineteenth century, when painters turned their attention to natural scenes as intrinsically valuable, the romantics tended to invest their scenery with human emotions and values and to see the natural only in a human frame of reference. They betray, however subtly, what critics have called the "pathetic fallacy," the tendency to read human values into nature and to sentimentalize it. Whenever Western painters have taken up the brush or chisel, they have revealed this abiding belief in a hierarchical existence in which the human ranks only slightly below the divine.

To see that this is not a universal penchant and to simultaneously see a portrait of the universe as experienced by another part of the human family, we might briefly turn to the Oriental wing of our art museum. In the art of the Far East we see few faces—an empress or two, a few high-ranking Buddhist monks at most. We see mainly landscapes, done in black ink on silk or paper, for just as portraiture and human events are the dominant Western concern, the landscape is dominant in Oriental art. Yet humans are there in the landscapes, along with their homes, occupations, and diversions. But if one were to walk quickly past the scrolls, these figures would be almost, or completely, overlooked, for they do not stand out in the paintings. In fact, no one part of the scene dominates the others. The scene is one of mountains, trees, a stream or lake, perhaps a small hut barely visible in the trees, and a small human figure or two. The mountains recede into the hazy distance, suggesting great spaces, and while the scene is tranquil and serene, there is nevertheless the strong suggestion of a living vitality, a breathing life. The viewer is struck by a sense of continuity among the various elements of the scene, in which all are united in an organic whole. The humans in the picture, which are almost always there, have their rightful place in this scene, but only their rightful place as one part of the whole. Nature here is not a background for man; man and nature are blended together harmoniously. Even this way of analyzing the scene distorts the situation; we see only being itself in its totality, "man" being merely one isolatable element of no more or less prominence than a tree or a bird. Are ye not of more worth than many sparrows? No.

These two examples of art reveal, I suggest, two different ways of understanding not only man's place in the total scheme of things, but the basic structure of existence in general. The humanistic or anthropocentric orientation of the first painting is clearly in sharp contrast with the landscape, assuming the status of a self-evident presupposition. The humanistic bias of the former also reflects a tacit assumption that being is organized in a hierarchical manner, in which some parts of existence—notably the divine and human—stand above other parts, with all the rights and privileges pertaining thereof. Man often resembles Warty Bliggens, the toad, in Don Marquis' poem:

> i met a toad
> the other day by the name
> of warty bliggens
> he was sitting under
> a toadstool
> feeling contented
> he explained that when the cosmos
> was created
> that toadstool was especially
> planned for his personal
> shelter from sun and rain
> thought out and prepared
> for him
> do not tell me
> said warty bliggens
> that there is not a purpose
> in the universe
> the thought is blasphemy
> a little more
> conversation revealed
> that warty bliggens
> considers himself to be
> the center of the said
> universe
> the earth exists
> to grow toadstools for him
> to sit under
> the sun to give him light
> by day and the moon
> and wheeling constellations
> to make beautiful
> the night for the sake of
> warty bliggens[1]

Historically there has been little doubt on the part of Western man that he does stand apart from, and superior to, all else. When he gazes out at the creation, he sees a reality which is primarily broken and fragmented, with none of the continuity and interrelatedness which we observed in the Chinese landscape, and of course this discontinuity, or alienation, exists mainly for him and his confrontation with the other. This would be of merely academic interest were it not for the fact that such a view is said to cause the individual to suffer greatly.

Now, while there seems to be a fundamental difference in the way Western and Eastern people regard experience, let it not be assumed that a Chinese or Japanese is born into the world with a vision of identity and interdependence. Buddhism was founded by an Indian and the Hua-yen school was a product of Chinese experience; both were taught to help Oriental people, who suffer from the same existential plight that Western people do. Human beings are basically the same in the manner in which they organize experience through recurrent training, learning to make sense out of what William James spoke of as a "blooming, buzzing confusion." However, Buddhism did arise in the East, indicating that there is a *tendency* to see things as described by Hua-yen. Conversely, the *tendency* in the West has been to analyze rather than unify, to discriminate rather than see all as one, to make distinctions rather than see all qualities within each datum of experience. But the truth of the matter is that the universe as described in Hua-yen documents is the world as seen by enlightened individuals, Buddhas, and not by ordinary folk of any race, time, or geographic area. Thus the Hua-yen vision is not at all self-evident, even to a Chinese philosopher. The message of Buddhism is claimed to be universal; since all men suffer in the same basic way, the cure is universally beneficial.

The Chinese landscapes described above can be thought of as plastic duplicates of Hua-yen philosophy, in the sense that both attempt to express a vision of the manner in which things exist. What is clear from both is that there is a great emphasis on the relatedness of things, and as was mentioned, this relationship is the dual one of identity and interdependence. This matter of relationship is extremely important, and perhaps the most important difference between the Hua-yen view of things and the ordinary view is that people ordinarily think and experience in terms of distinct, separate *entities*, while Hua-yen conceives of experience primarily in terms of the *relationships* between these same entities. It is simply a question of fundamental, basic reality; is it separate parcels of matter (or mental objects) or is it relationship? It is interesting in this regard to see that a great number of Western physicists have now drawn the conclusion, based on the implications of Einstein's theories, that relationship is the more fundamental. As one physicist has remarked, if all the matter in the universe less one bundle of matter ceased to exist, the mass of the remaining parcel of matter (and hence its existence) would be reduced to nothing, the implication being that mass is a function of total environment and dependent on it.[2] Nonetheless, in the seventh century, Fa-tsang and other Hua-yen masters taught that to exist in any sense at all means to exist in dependence on the other, which is infinite in number. Nothing exists truly in and of itself, but requires everything to be what it is.

Previously, in examining the relationship existing among ten coins, it was said that any one coin is identical with all the other coins. The reader has undoubtedly heard of this business of identity before, Oh yes, the Mysterious East has this obsession with Identity. We smile to think of the yogi walking through the jungle meditating on the sameness of things and being pounced upon and eaten by a real, unmystical tiger. So much for identity, we say, in the belief that we have disposed of any nonsense about identity. Or, like the cynic in Orwell's *Animal Farm*, we may grant that things are all equal, but some things are more equal than others. Things seem to be very unequal, radically nonidentical. But the Hua-yen masters were not mystics, and while agreeing that there were men and tigers, eaters and eaten, they could insist on identity anyway. Let us turn to another example of identity in an attempt to see in what way things are just what they are and yet identical.

We might take the example of a human body as a kind of organic whole similar to the totality analyzed by Hua-yen. Here too we can agree that there are distinctions in form and function among the constituents of the whole body. My ears do not look like my toes, and I cannot see with my elbow. Ears detect sounds, my stomach digests food, my nose detects odors and helps me to breathe. We do not confuse the parts; we know where everything is and what it does. It is equally evident that what we call the body is an organism made up of all these parts, and normally the parts do not exist apart from the body. (The body analogy breaks down in this matter because a toe can be severed from the body and continue to exist. However, taking the cosmos as a totality, this would not happen, since the disappearance of something from the totality would be tantamount to its having become a nonentity.) If we now look into the relationship between any one part of the body and the whole body, it will be obvious that we are really discussing the relationship between this one part and all other parts, whether considered individually or collectively.

Let us examine the place of the nose, being prominent and therefore seeming to offer itself for inspection. In what sense is it identical with my body or with any other part of the body? The Hua-yen argument is really very simple; what we call the whole is nothing apart from the individuals which make up that whole. Thus the nose, in being integrated perfectly into the configuration we call a body, not only acts as a condition without which there could be no body, but in fact becomes or is the body. I can therefore point to my nose and say, "This is my body," and there will be no disagreement, with the possible exception that someone might say, "It is only a part of your body." This is true; it is a part of my body, but at the same time it is my body. To insist that it is *only* a part is to fall into a fallacious view of the whole as an independent and subsisting entity to which parts belong. The bell tower on the Riverside campus of the University of California is not something which is added to an already existent campus. It is the campus. Thus the part and the whole in this sense are one and the same thing, for what we identify as a part is merely an abstraction from a unitary whole.

But in what way can it be said that the nose is identical with my left elbow? We may understand that in a sense a part is identical with the whole as a whole, but identifying part with part raises difficulties, for the two parts look different, are spatially distinct, and perform different functions. The postulation of identity does not remove these distinctions, and Hua-yen insists that not only are things both identical *and* different, but, paradoxically, that they are identical *because* they are different. In other words, to have the body I now have, I need a nose which is between my eyes and has the office of detecting odors, an elbow which bends in a certain way, allowing me to write and the like, a heart in my chest which pumps blood, and so on. If everything was literally a nose, I would be just one immense nose; in fact, I could not be "me" for even one second. Thus each individual is required in its own unique form, with its own unique function, to act as a condition for the whole in question. The identity of the nose and the left elbow consists in their identity as *conditions* for the whole. Therefore, while the two are different, they are the same; in fact, they are identical precisely because they are different. Seen in this light, then, when the nose is understood for what it is, the whole body is known; when we know the nature of the body, we know what the nose is. For this reason, Hua-yen can say that ten thousand Buddhas can be seen preaching on the tip of a single hair. In other words, the one truth which is common of all things (ten thousand Buddhas) is evident in the tip of the hair once we know its place in the whole.

The reader is bound, at this point, to interpose in exasperation, "Very well, they are all the same *as conditions*, but nevertheless, life and death don't appear to be the same to me!" Certainly they seem different. One moment the loved one is talking with us, his cheeks pink with life, loving and caring for us, and the next moment he lies still, pale in death, never more to laugh, love, or care again. Is there no difference? Does nothing happen when the hard-headed, practical tiger eats the mystical yogi?

Yes, of course something happens, the Hua-yen Buddhist agrees that something does. The yogi really dies and becomes part of the tiger (though this is not the kind of identity insisted upon by Hua-yen). Now, we may go out and shoot the tiger so he won't eat any more people, but we are still left confronting the question of the place of tigers in the world, and our attitude here is going to determine whether our own private existence is going to be a success or a failure. It is the human habit to reject such things as hungry tigers, or their equivalents— cancer, bullets, or the slow, insidious, but equally effective tiger of old age. We would have nothing but sunshine, sweet wine, eternal youth, and endless satisfactory amours. Intellectually we know that tigers are real and do exist, but emotionally we reject them with fear and loathing, and we would rather that they did not exist. They are somehow intruders in the sacred circle of life, foreign agents sent to subvert our happiness. They are antilife. It is this very picking and choosing which brings back upon ourselves anxiety, fear, and turmoil, for by dividing up the one unitary existence into two parts, the good and the bad, we distort the reality which is the one unitary existence. That is, we blind ourselves to the fact that existence in its totality is both life *and* death, success *and* failure, health *and* sickness. Tigers are not foreign intruders but facts of life.

Both life and death are part of the one everchanging process we call being (which is really a "becoming") and thus both are conditions for that being. To see things in a totalistic perspective means to transcend a small, pathetic subjectivity and see all the pernicious, vexing contraries harmonized within the whole. As D.T. Suzuki said in his commentary on Basho's *haiku*

> Lice, fleas—
> The horse pissing
> Beside my pillow

the real world is a world of lice as well as butterflies, horse piss as well as vintage champagne, and to the person who has truly realized this, one is as good as the other.[3] To insist otherwise is to make an impious demand of existence which it is unwilling and unable to satisfy. The "ugly" things of life exist, and the only question is how we are to confront them. The romantic hero smashing himself to pieces against the stone wall of necessity has never found favor in Asian literature.

This matter of identity can be explored in more depth if we turn to the matter of interdependence again, for the two relationships are so inextricably related themselves that one cannot be understood without the other. In returning to the nose, let us examine it in its dynamic relationship with the body-totality. Now, this humble organ is, according to Hua-yen, the total cause for the rest of the body. Since, as was pointed out, the "rest" is an assemblage of parts, this means that the nose causes my right elbow, my left knee, and so on. This is, admittedly, a highly unusual way of looking at a nose, and it is true that if in this analysis of cause and result we stopped completely with the assertion that the nose causes the body, this would be a very questionable assertion indeed. Moving from this example to the Hua-yen cosmos, this would be tantamount to saying that a drop of water in the Nile River is the cause for the whole universe. Mysticism indeed! But the issue of one sole causal agent is not being discussed here, and, in fact, part of the function of Hua-yen thought is to destroy the fiction of a sole causal agent. The apparent absurdity of arguing that the nose causes the rest of my body arises from the sheer necessity of examining the relationship of *each* part of the whole to the whole in a linear manner, one part at a time in sequence. If we move to another part of the body, the left index finger, let us say, we can now assert that the finger is the cause for the body. This does not cancel out the causal function of the nose; the reality of the situation is that any part can be said to assume the role of total cause when the relationship is examined purely from the point of view of the one part being examined. At this point, it might be assumed that the Hua-yen masters are making a rather commonplace observance, that a whole is the result of the collaboration of many individual parts each exerting its own partial causal power. However, this is not the case, and Fa-tsang, in his *Hua-yen i-ch'eng chiao i fen-ch'i chang*, says that if this were the case,

> there would be the errors of annihilationism and eternalism. If [each part] does not wholly cause [the whole] to be made and only exerts partial power, then each condition would only have partial power. They would consist only of many individual partial powers and would not make one whole, which is annihilationism. . . . Also, if [the part] does not wholly create [the whole], then when one [part] is removed, the [whole] should remain. However, since the whole is not formed, then you should understand that the [whole] is not formed by the partial power [of a condition] but by its total power.[4]

Thus according to the Hua-yen school, the part exerts *total power* in the formation of a particular whole.

In a later chapter devoted to intercausality alone, the problem of sole causal power residing in any individual part will be discussed in more detail. Here, in a general description of the Hua-yen world view, it will suffice to say that when we move to every part of the body, to every organ, limb, cell, or subcellular particle, and in each case analyze the relationship of that part to the whole body, it can be said that that part of the whole is *the* sole cause for the whole. When referring to causality, Hua-yen is not making the naive assertion that first there is, let us say, a nose, and then later the rest of the body comes into existence as a result of the prior condition of the nose. Time is not involved, nor is there a question of production of a result from a cause in a progressive series of events. The real question concerns the relationship existing between simultaneously existing individuals. Whether a totality is composed of two parts, a million parts, or an infinity of parts, causality in the sense meant by Hua-yen refers to a relationship among present entities.

The totality we have been looking at is nothing more than a number of simultaneously existing individuals, and since the relationship of support and supported always exists between any one individual and all other individuals, or the whole, it would seem clear that not only does the individual support the whole, but upon a more complete investigation it can be seen that what is a cause or support from one point of view is result or the supported from another. The categories of support and supported, or cause and result, are completely fluid and interchangeable, becoming either as the point of view shifts. It is the necessity of point of view which in fact obscures the real status of the individuals which comprise the whole. They are all simultaneously cause and result, or support and supported, for this is precisely the picture of existence which Hua-yen hopes to describe: a universe which is nothing but the complete mutual cooperation of the entities which make it up.

It may be well to try to clarify the sense in which Hua-yen uses the term "cause" at this point. The description of the intercausal or interdependent nature of the parts of the body illustrates the magnitude of the relationships as well as the nature of that relationship, but the meanings of "cause," "condition," "support," and other terms have not been discussed at much length. As has already been mentioned, "cause" is not used here in the popularly understood sense of a temporal sequence of events in which if an antecedent event is present, a subsequent event will occur. Perhaps the Hua-yen use of the term will become clearer if we resort to a model of an even simpler kind. Let us take a tripod. If we bind three poles together near one end and then stand the three poles up on outspread legs, the tripod will remain standing. Here the tripod is a whole, which is of course composed of parts. If, now, one of the poles is removed, the other two poles will topple over. This toppling action is not meant, however, to show what happens to the whole when a part is removed, but rather shows that in order to be *that* whole it needs this one pole. Obviously the universe does not collapse when one individual member dies, but it is no longer *that* particular whole it was when the individual survived. Now, if we label the three poles *a*, *b*, and *c* and remove pole *a*, the falling of the remaining two poles shows that from the point of view of *a*, it has complete power to form the tripod. However, if we turn our attention to pole *b*, now that pole, from the new point of view, is said to be completely responsible for the whole tripod. What has happened to *a*? Seen from the point of view of pole *b*, it is result, or that which is supported. Since a tripod is three interdependent poles, each of the three parts is simultaneously acting as cause or support for the whole tripod and yet is indubitably part of a whole which is being supported.

It is to be admitted that the term "cause" is being used in an unusual manner in these examples, since what is evident is that these are all examples of what might better be called interdependency or mutual conditionedness. Yet, Fa-tsang and other Hua-yen masters do use the word "cause," and the Hua-yen universe is a universe of self-causation. The traditional term to describe such a situation is *fa-chiai yüan-ch'i*, which seems to be a translation of the Sanskrit *dharma-dhātu pratītya-samutpāda*, translated either as the "interdependent arising of the universe," or, perhaps better, the "interdependent arising which is the universe," since all that exists is part of the one great scheme of interdependency. Bertrand Russell said that the only reasonable definition of cause would be the sum total of all existent conditions, in the sense that any event will occur unless any one of the available conditions fails. It is in this sense that we should understand the Hua-yen use of the word, for in the Hua-yen universe, the individual will *be*, and will perform its function, unless some other individual withdraws its support.

One of the most important implications of such a view is that every single thing in the universe comes to have an important place in the scheme of things. In the "Great Barn," every rafter, shingle, and nail is important, for where can we find a barn apart from these things? This apparently insignificant shingle I see there in the building is a necessary condition for the barn, and in fact, it *is* the barn. Yet, what do we mean by "shingle"? It is not a shingle outside the context of the barn of which it is a part, for "shingle" only has meaning in its proper context. It is true that there is no building without this little shingle, but it is equally evident that "shingle" has neither existence nor meaning outside the barn of which it is a part. They make and define each other.

To make one more analogy in a rather long series of analogies, existence is something like an old-fashioned American square dance. In the square dance, what I am and what I do are completely defined by my inclusion in the square dance, for obviously I am nothing apart from it. My being, and my office, can be seen as being nothing but functions of the dance in which I exist. However, where is the square dance without me, and "I" am every member of the dance? I am the square dance. Thus we have a profound, crucial relationship here; that

I am, and that I am defined in a certain way, is completely dependent on the *other* individuals who comprise the dance, but this dance itself has no existence apart from the dancer. The Buddhist, in viewing things as being interdependent in this manner, comes to have, ideally, a profound feeling of gratitude and respect for things, however humble they may appear to people who do not share his understanding, for in some manner that eludes the rest of us, he is aware that what he is depends utterly upon them.

Having taken this brief look at the doctrine of interdependence, we may now return to the matter of identity, as perhaps more problematic than the matter of interdependence. Yet, there is finally no real problem, because "identity" is only another way of saying "interdependent"; they are one and the same. The point to the doctrine of interdependence is that things exist *only* in interdependence, for things do not exist in their own right. In Buddhism, this manner of existence is called "emptiness" (Sanskrit *śūnyatā*). Buddhism says that things are empty in the sense that they are absolutely lacking in a self-essence (*svabhāva*) by virtue of which things would have an independent existence. In reality, their existence derives strictly from interdependence. If things possessed essences or substances of a metaphysical nature, then there truly would be real, ultimate differences between things. However, if each experiential datum, whether material or mental, derives its existence and meaning purely through its dependence on everything else, then it is not ultimately unique at all, but must be seen as identical with everything else in its emptiness. Thus to be identical with everything else means to share in the universal interdependence, or intercausality, of all that exists. If the reader objects that he still perceives a vast difference between good and evil, or Buddhas and ordinary folk, or life and death, he need not be surprised, for to be human means to perceive these differences. However, the Buddha insisted that to be attached to these meanings in such a manner brought disaster to the individual. It is the perennial teaching of Buddhism that such attachment will fill his heart with desire and loathing, make his life a ceaseless hell of turmoil (*duḥkha*), madden him, and finally send him to his grave confused, bitter, and afraid.

Identity can be thought of as the static relationship among things, while interdependence is the dynamic relationship; they are two sides of the same coin, and both are alternate ways of saying that all is empty (*sarvam śūnyam*). It is on the basis of this doctrine of emptiness that Hua-yen insists on a totalistic view of things. Totalism has two meanings. First, it means that all things are contained in each individual. The nose, in its identity and interdependence with the rest of the body, takes in the whole body, for whatever is true in the ultimate sense concerning the nose is also true of the whole body. If we know reality in the form of one phenomenon, then we know all of reality. It is for this reason that Hua-yen can make the seemingly outrageous claim that the whole universe is contained in a grain of sand. However, not only does the one contain the all, but at the same time, the all contains the one, for the individual is completely integrated into its environment.

Second, totalism refers to a manner of experiencing events in which room is allowed for all kinds of events, and in which nothing is excluded as alien or "bad," as was discussed earlier. This is difficult to accept for the person unaccustomed to Eastern thought, for it demands of him that he make room not grudgingly or fatalistically, but joyously and with profound gratitude, for the horse urine and lice that do in fact coexist with fine champagne and beautiful butterflies. The totalistic view sees these as no less real, and no less wonderful, once we have transcended a petty, partial view of existence in which our comfort and unslakable thirst determine what has and has not a right to exist. In the totalistic universe, which is one organic body of interacting parts, it is an act of self-defeating madness to insist on a never-ending diet of vintage champagne, sunshine, and laughter, and to insist vehemently and with no small amount of hubris that urine, darkness, and tears be banished forever. In every contest, there has to be of necessity both a winner and a loser (granting an occasional draw), and all that Hua-yen asks is that we realize, and appreciate, the fact that we cannot ever have one without the other. The partial view would have only one or the other; the totalistic view sees that the two always go together.

The totalistic world as described by Hua-yen is a living body in which each cell derives its life from all the other cells, and in return gives life to those many others. Like the human body, the Hua-yen universe is ever changing, for in it there is not one thing which is static and unchanging, unless it is the law of perpetual change itself. It is an incredible stream of activity wherein when one circumstance alters, everything alters with it. "Do I dare to eat a peach?" asks one of T.S. Eliot's characters, and the question of action becomes an extremely delicate one to the individual who sees the fantastic interaction of things. Thus in a universe which is pure fluidity, or process, no act can but have an effect on the whole, just as a pebble tossed into a pool sends waves out to the farthest shore and stirs the very bottom. This is hard to see. We can comprehend how a modification in one small part of our body can affect the total organism, but we find it hard to believe that the enlightenment of one monk under a tree in India somehow enlightens us all, or, conversely, that my own intransigent ignorance is a universal ignorance. However, if we can comprehend that the greater whole of which the body is a part is no less organic, and no less interrelated, such an idea is not so unlikely. At that point, the moral life as conceived by Buddhism becomes possible.

University students today do not find the Buddhist concepts of emptiness and interdependent existence (which are the same thing) difficult to understand, as they might have been a generation ago and more. Much more conversant, if even in an elementary way, with scientific and philosophical trends, they can see fairly easily that the very old Western assumptions about substances, selves, agents, and the like, are no longer tenable, or are at least open to serious doubt. Their intellectual world is a different one from that of even the previous generation. They feel much more at home with such startling concepts as the unified field and the ecosphere. They have begun to appreciate, however dimly, that in some real sense, everything is alive and exerting its influence on everything else, that even dead things are alive. They agree with the Cheyenne chief Old Lodge Skins in the novel *Little Big Man*, who, asked if he hates white people, says,

> "No. . . . But now I understand them. I no longer believe they are fools or crazy. I know now that they do not drive away the buffalo by mistake or accidentally set fire to the prairie with their fire-wagon or rub out Human Beings because of misunderstanding. No, they *want* to do these things, and they succeed in doing them. They are a powerful people." He took something from his beaded belt at that point and, stroking it, said: "The Human Beings believe that everything is alive: not only men and animals but also water and earth and stones and also the dead things from them like this hair. The person from whom this hair came is bald on the Other Side because I now own his scalp. This is the *way things are*.
>
> "But white people believe that everything is dead: stones, earth, animals, and people, even their own people. And if, in spite of that, things persist in trying to live, white people will rub them out."[5]

We have for a long time smiled at such assertions as being the superstitions of "primitive" people, preliterate, simple folk who have a tendency to invest everything with spirits. Yet people far more sophisticated (according to our usual standards) have said as much. Faraday, over a hundred years ago, made the startling remark that an electric charge must be considered to exist everywhere, and Alfred North Whitehead, commenting on this statement, paraphrased it by saying that "the modification of the electromagnetic field at every point of space at each instant owing to the past history of each electron is another way of stating the same fact."[6] Faraday, the American Indian, and the Buddhists of the Hua-yen are all, in their own way, making the observation that nature is not at all dead, but rather is most vital. It is certainly not a case of animism or spiritism, but, whatever may be the basis, a realization that even things commonly thought to be dead or inanimate exert a continual, crucial influence on each other.

The work of earlier physicists such as Faraday and Maxwell, and later men such as Einstein, as well as Whitehead with his process philosophy, and others, have all laid the groundwork for an entirely new understanding of the nature of existence, and this understanding is gradually beginning to filter down to the layman. Thus, as I remarked earlier, the intellectual grasp of such Buddhist concepts as emptiness and interdependence has become much easier and much more prevalent, so that the university student is not absolutely baffled by these ideas. So much that is in the air in Western thought coincides in general outline with Hua-yen cosmology that what might have once passed for bad thinking by Oriental "mystics" can now be discussed seriously.

My concluding point is that intellectual grasp is not enough, according to all that the old Buddhist thinkers have had to say. They did not intend their treatises to be mere theoretical exercises, to be read, understood, and filed away in the great dust bin of the mind. The Hua-yen vision was first of all meant to tantalize the reader and lure him to *realize* (i.e., to *make real* in his everyday experience) what had been only theory. To realize the Hua-yen universe means to go beyond an intellectual grasp of the system to a *lived experience* of things existing in this manner, for the Hua-yen world view is nothing if not a lived reality. To live this reality in turn means to alter drastically one's moral and ethical stance as they relate to the infinite other. The final chapter of this book will examine some of the implications of the Hua-yen world view for practice and ethics, but here, in conclusion, a story told by a Buddhist priest may give some idea of what it means to live the Hua-yen vision.

> That I have been able to establish myself as well as I have has been totally because of my teacher's guidance. It was customary for him to visit the shrines of various guardians, placed around the grounds of the temple, every day after the morning service. One morning while he was making his rounds, he discovered a single chopstick in a drain. He brought it back, called me to his room, held out the chopstick to me and asked, "What is this?" I replied, "It is a chopstick." "Yes, this is a chopstick. Is it unusable?" he asked further. "No," I said, "It is still usable." "Quite so," he said, "And yet I found it in a drain with other scraps. That is to say, you have taken the life of this chopstick. You may know the proverb, 'He who kills another digs two graves.' Since you have killed this chopstick, you will be killed by

it." Spending four or five hours on this incident he told me how I should practice. At that time I was seven or eight years old. His guidance at that time really soaked in. From that time on, I became very careful and meticulous about everything.[7]

In the Hua-yen universe, where everything interpenetrates in identity and interdependence, where everything needs everything else, what is there which is not valuable? To throw away even a single chopstick as worthless is to set up a hierarchy of values which in the end will kill us in a way in which no bullet can. In the Hua-yen universe, everything counts.

2

The Hua-yen School

The universe of the wonderful jewel net of Indra described in the previous chapter is the teaching of a school of Buddhism which arose and flourished in China in the T'ang dynasty (618–907), although its intellectual roots are far more ancient. This form of Buddhism, called Hua-yen (pronounced Hwah-yen, the last syllable rhyming with "men"), looked for its inspiration to a Buddhist scripture of Indian, or partly Indian, origin named the *Avataṁsaka Sūtra*. Hua-yen is the Chinese translation of *Avataṁsaka*, meaning "Flower Ornament." The school or sect of Hua-yen took its name from the scripture which served as the basis for its own special concern.

When I refer to the "school" or "sect" of Hua-yen, I am not suggesting that Hua-yen was anything like a sect in the Western tradition, for there was no feeling of sectarian exclusiveness or rivalry involved in belonging to this tradition. Hua-yen, like the other Chinese scholastic traditions such as T'ien-t'ai, San-lun, and Fa-hsiang, was more in the order of an academic tradition, devoted to systematizing, studying, and propagating one particular aspect of the whole of Buddhist thought. A monk who was associated with the Hua-yen school might very well devote his entire life to the study and exegesis of the *Avataṁsaka Sūtra*, writing many learned treatises on the complexities and niceties of that scripture, but he also very well might practice a form of meditation such as was taught by the new Ch'an school, or he might recite the name of Amito, the Buddha, as was done in the Pure Land tradition, and he probably would have an extensive knowledge of other forms of Buddhism as well. The fifth patriarch of Hua-yen, Tsung-mi (779–840), for example, was simultaneously a Hua-yen master and a Ch'an master.

Hua-yen is an example of a peculiarity of Chinese Buddhism, in which traditions of scholarship and teaching arose and were centered around the study of one or more Indian scriptural or commentarial works. For instance, the T'ien-t'ai tradition was primarily concerned with the *Saddharmpuṇḍarīka Sūtra*, the Fa-hsiang concerned itself with the *Vijñaptimātratā-siddhi*, and the She-lun school concentrated on the *Mahāyānasaṁgraha-śāstra*. It was as if in the West a group of Christians were to decide that there was something special about the Book of Ecclesiastes and start a tradition of study, exegesis, and commentary centering almost exclusively around this one part of the whole scriptural tradition. They would still be Christians, with by and large the same beliefs and practices as other Christians, but because of their primary concern with Ecclesiastes, they would become known as the "Ecclesiastesians" or the "Ecclesiastes School." This is what the men did who began the Hua-yen tradition. Their work centered around one scripture, which for them was not necessarily more correct than any other Buddhist scripture, but rather was more complete. Though in time it was considered to be a distinct form of Buddhism, at all times there was more to link them with the whole larger body of Buddhism than there was to separate them. Though the Hua-yen masters are distinguished by their scholarly work, they seem to have been pious Buddhists involved in the practical life of Buddhism also.

Much of the history of the *Avataṁsaka Sūtra*, as with many other Mahayana Buddhist scriptures, is still unclear. What does seem clear is that most of the separate chapters which now constitute the larger work were composed in Central Asia or even in China.[1] Though the work was translated into Chinese from Sanskrit by Buddhabhadra in about 420, only two parts are now wholly extant in their Sanskrit originals, and with the exception of a brief quotation of another chapter in the *Śikṣāsamuccaya*, there is no mention in Indian Buddhist literature of any other of the many chapters of the *Avataṁsaka*.[2] This, coupled with the appearance in the sutra of Central Asian and Chinese place names, would seem to indicate that much of the sutra was composed outside of India.[3]

Two very important portions of the sutra do, however, exist in Sanskrit. The chapter called the "Ten Stages" (*Daśabhūmika*) has apparently also existed from the time of its composition in the second century of the Christian era as an independent sutra. The Sanskrit original was edited some years ago by Johannes Rahder, and it bears a strong resemblance to the Chinese of Buddhabhadra's translation.[4] Since it first appeared in India, this important text has generally been the standard in any discussion of the stages a Bodhisattva passes through from the beginning of his religious career up to final enlightenment. The Hua-yen school was interested both in this description of the Bodhisattva's progress and in several passages which say that the whole world is nothing but Mind. The interest of Hua-yen in this text was also excited because of Vasubandhu's commentary on it, which contained an interpretation of the relationship of the ten stages to each other which became part of later Hua-yen philosophy. In a way, the

Daśabhūmika is one of the most crucial chapters of the larger sutra, because it gives an epitome of the larger structure, and there is reason to believe that the larger structure of the *Avataṁsaka* itself was inspired by the *Daśabhūmika*. Despite its eventual inclusion in the larger sutra, it has always maintained a separate existence and importance, and with the advent of the work of Bodhiruci in the sixth century, a separate Chinese school, the Ti-lun, arose which was exclusively devoted to the study of the sutra and its commentary.

The other chapter for which a complete Sanskrit original exists is the *Gaṇḍa-vyūha*, a very large sutra in itself which now constitutes the final portion of the *Avataṁsaka*. It also dates from the second century. The Sanskrit text was edited by Hokei Idzumi and D.T. Suzuki.[5] This sutra describes the wandering of the youth Sudhana, who, in his search for enlightenment, travels about speaking to various people who can help enlighten him. He receives this teaching from fifty-two people before he perceives the truth. Sudhana is a Buddhist Everyman, and his indefatigable search is another epitome of the long journey to enlightenment which the *Avataṁsaka* describes in almost excruciating detail. Suzuki has spoken of it as one of the most dazzling works ever conceived by *homo religiosus*. It is, in fact, similar in many ways to Dante's *Divine Comedy* and Bunyan's *Pilgrim's Progress*, but without their terror, superstition, and idolatry. When, at the end of his epic journey, Sudhana is ushered into the Tower of Maitreya and shown the truth, it is the world of the Buddhas, which transcends ignorance, hatred, and desire. It is tempting to give a résumé of this astonishing work here, but it would take us beyond the scope of this chapter. However, Suzuki's *Essays in Zen Buddhism* (Third Series) contains an excellent résumé. The Hua-yen was interested in this work not only for its portrayal of the life of the Bodhisattva, but also for its rich material on the harmonious and totalistic nature of existence.

There are several theories concerning the composition of the *Avataṁsaka*, but students of this text are agreed on several points. Somewhere in Central Asia, probably in the region of Khotan, a single compiler or several compilers, probably inspired by the *Daśabhūmika* and *Gaṇḍavyūha*, assembled a number of independent sutras in such a manner that the finished work gave a very detailed description of the progress of the Bodhisattva from the time he began his practice up to his achievement of enlightenment. In some instances, new sutras may have been composed to fill crucial gaps in this preconceived structure. The finished work was then translated into Chinese in sixty volumes, by Buddha-bhadra, in 420; it was later translated by Śikṣānanda, in eighty volumes, in about 699, and the *Gaṇḍavyūha* section was separately translated in forty volumes by Prajñā, in the late eighth century.

Reading this mammoth work is, to put it mildly, an unforgettable experience.

Buddhabhadra's translation, for instance, comprises thirty-four chapters and contains over 400 pages of Chinese in the Japanese *Taishō Shinshū Daizōkyō* edition with each page comprising over 1,500 Chinese characters. But the sheer volume of words is nowhere near as formidable as the content itself; like most Mahayana Buddhist works, everything is done on a gargantuan scale. If one simile is good, ten are always much better. The reader is staggered by the loving description of scenery, down to the numbers of leaves on the trees, with their configuration and coloring; with the descriptions of perfumed trees and golden lotuses, singing birds, clouds that emit wonderful odors and sounds, varieties of clothing and jewels, the long lists of names of Bodhisattvas and Śrāvakas assembled to hear the teaching, more numerous than all the sands in a million Ganges Rivers, and so on for page after page. Moreover, the sutra is a vehicle for many of the more abstruse and subtle doctrines of Mahayana Buddhism, such as those of "Mind-only" and "Emptiness," not to mention that which became the special province of Hua-yen, the doctrine of the infinitely repeated intercausality and identity of all phenomena. There is a great amount of drama and color in the *Avataṁsaka*, but it is all there to serve the overriding concern of Buddhism, to show man what he must do to become free, and what freedom is.

The richness and profundity of the sutra began to attract the attention of Chinese Buddhists from the time of its first translation. There is much in the sutra to attract a pious and zealous Buddhist, but primarily the attraction lies in the doctrine of identity and intercausality, which is unique to this one sutra. An academic tradition of study, exegesis, and teaching gradually grew up around the sutra, but it was several centuries after its translation before there existed an independent school as such. During the period from its translation in the first decade of the fifth century up to the early T'ang, the tradition centered around the scholarly work of individual monks belonging to various other academic traditions, as well as the work of schools like the Ti-lun and She-lun, each working on various problems and contributing their insights to what was later to be recognized as a separate school. Some of the other traditions, such as Ti-lun and She-lun, became absorbed into Hua-yen, because the latter thoroughly encompassed their own special areas of interest. Even the three men who are considered now to have been the first three patriarchs of Hua-yen—Tu-shun, Chih-yen, and Fa-tsang—were not themselves conscious of belonging to some distinct school called "Hua-yen"; it was not until the time of Ch'eng-kuan, the fourth patriarch (783–839), that a separate school was recognized and given the name of Hua-yen.

I have, from time to time, used the word "patriarch" with reference to leading figures in the development of Hua-yen, but these early figures in the history of the school did not consider themselves to be anything like patriarchs of a new school. They were just Buddhists who were especially attracted to one particular scripture. The patriarchal tradition of Hua-yen, like that of Ch'an and other Chinese forms of Buddhism, was established much later than the time of the "patriarchs," when some need arose to base the teachings of the school squarely on an unbroken line of masters stretching far back into Chinese history and often beyond to a line of Indian masters who in turn were descended in authority from the Buddha himself. The conferring of the exalted title of "master" or spokesman for a school was thus often made long after the life of the master in question. In some patriarchal traditions, there is occasionally some real transmission of doctrine from master to disciple, but often the lineage is in great part fictional.

In the case of Hua-yen, Tu-shun (557–640), the acknowledged first patriarch, was given that title after the time of Tsung-mi (779–840), the fifth patriarch, who himself is recognized as being a Ch'an master as well as Hua-yen master. However, there is real doubt as to whether Tu-shun should be considered a Hua-yen master at all. Some scholars have suggested Chih-cheng (602–668) as having a better right to the title, since he was the teacher of Chih-yen, who is recognized as the second master. Some have suggested that Chih-yen himself was the first master of Hua-yen.[6] Nevertheless, the present accepted history according to Hua-yen has Tu-shun as first master, Chih-yen as the second, and Fa-tsang the third. After the time of Fa-tsang (643–712), apparently a monk named Hui-yüan was recognized as the foremost scholar of Hua-yen thought, but the later creators of the Hua-yen patriarchal lineage apparently felt that his interpretation of Fatsang's system was not orthodox enough. Therefore, he was made a "nonperson"; i.e., he was denied the title of fourth patriarch, and Ch'eng-kuan, even though born twenty-six years after the death of Fa-tsang and therefore by no means a real heir to Fa-tsang's teaching, was given the title of patriarch. The patchy nature of patriarchal lineages is further evidenced by the fact that Tsung-mi could be considered a patriarch in both Hua-yen and Ch'an simultaneously.

The study of Hua-yen continued, of course, after the time of Tsung-mi, but the times were hard for Buddhism. In 845, the great persecution of Buddhism by the Emperor Wu brought Hua-yen, as well as most other forms of Chinese Buddhism, to an end, as far as creative vitality is concerned. Only the nonphilosophical forms such as Ch'an and Pure Land continued to develop and flourish. Some useful commentaries on Hua-yen treatises were composed during the Sung dynasty and later, but by that time, Hua-yen had ceased to exist as an independent entity, and Tsung-mi is the last of the Hua-yen masters. But for that matter, with the intricate and difficult works of Fa-tsang, Chinese Buddhist philosophical work had really reached its high point, and perhaps not much more was possible. Part of the reason for the decline of Hua-yen, as well as T'ien-t'ai, San-lun, She-lun, Fa-hsiang, and other academic traditions, was that they stressed a very high level of intellectual activity, and in limiting their appeal to the very small number of monks with the talent and taste for abstruse philosophy, they denied themselves the broad base of mass support required to maintain a tradition in need of money, land, books, and other material resources. There was, of course, no moral support either, so that Wu did not hesitate to squash these schools, destroying the monastery-university complexes, defrocking the monks, and appropriating the wealth of the schools. With no popular support and without the active support of the emperor, Hua-yen could no longer exist. The tradition continued to live in Japan, where it was imported earlier, as one of the famous six schools of Nara, but it is safe to say that there was never any real creative vitality in the Japanese school. In Japan, Hua-yen (or Kegon, as it is pronounced there) itself was in turn eclipsed by the great Tendai and Shingon schools of the Heian period.

The above story of the fortunes of Hua-yen may give the reader the impression that Hua-yen never amounted to much in the overall history of Buddhism. This would be an incorrect assessment of the influence of Hua-yen thought. As long as there is a Mahayana tradition of Buddhism, Hua-yen thought will continue to guide and inspire the seeker, for, as Hua-yen has always claimed, it was the historical mission of the school to try to present in its fullest and most perfect form that vision of the truth which is presumably the content of the enlightenment experience. Hua-yen had accomplished this mission in two ways. First, it had taken many different strands of Buddhist thought and brought them together in the form of a grand syncretism. Hua-yen created no new school of philosophy. Admittedly, even triumphantly syncretic, Hua-yen thinkers saw their task as that of being able to see the interrelationships between different schools of Buddhist thought and reassembling them to form their real whole. This can be a risky enterprise if there is very little real common ground among the various elements. Imagine someone trying to tack together the philosophies of Aquinas, Bishop Berkeley, Marx, and Wittgenstein. The result would be a mere patchwork, because each philosophy is largely discontinuous with the others, despite certain common presuppositions. However, Hua-yen could achieve a real syncretism because each different philosophical form of Buddhism is only part of the larger whole, and the study of any one aspect is no more isolated from its context than is the brain specialist's concern isolated from the more general concern for the total organism. It was the peculiar mission of Hua-yen to try, on a scale more vast and to a degree more satisfying than any other school of Buddhism, to reassemble all the apparently separate, diverse threads of Buddhist thought and weave them into a seamless whole.

Second, along with its syncretic effort, Hua-yen came to serve as the philosophical basis for the other schools of Buddhism more concerned with practice and realization. Thus not only is there no mutual exclusiveness at all between Hua-yen and Ch'an, but they are mutually complementary in a most profound and organic way. The Chinese have a saying: "Hua-yen for philosophy, Ch'an for practice." This does not imply a choice, but rather the interrelationship of the two. As D.T. Suzuki remarked, Hua-yen is the philosophy of Zen and Zen is the practice of Hua-yen.[7] Put another way, the picture of existence presented by Hua-yen is the universe experienced in Zen enlightenment. Without the practice and realization of Zen, Hua-yen philosophy remains mere intellectual fun, never a vibrant reality. Hua-yen, in turn, serves as an intriguing lure to the practitioner, a stimulus to effort, and a promise of a vision undreamed of in our more common hours. For these two reasons, Hua-yen is far from insignificant in the history of Buddhism. A third reason lies in the fact that it inspired some rather impressive art in China, Japan, and Java, but this lies outside the scope of this book.[8]

The syncretistic efforts of Hua-yen were so comprehensive that they managed to include not only most of what was significant in Buddhist thought, but much of what might be considered the characteristic features of indigenous Chinese thought as well. These native Chinese ideas are those usually associated with the philosophical Taoist traditions of Lao-tzu, Chuang-tzu, and the Neo-taoists. It is doubtful that the architects of Hua-yen, such as Chih-yen and Fa-tsang, deliberately incorporated these Taoist elements into their system; rather, they were Chinese who had what might be called "pictures" in their minds of how reality was constructed, and these pictures tended to influence subsequent modes of thinking. They were presuppositions of the most vital form, fundamental symbol systems by means of which experience was ordered.

First of all, there is the persistent, characteristic tendency on the part of people like Fa-tsang to take what might be called a totalistic view of existence. We first notice this tendency in earlier Taoist literature, particularly in the writings of Chuang-tzu and the later Neo-taoists. For instance, we find in Chuang-tzu's teachings the following:

> By what is the Tao hidden that there should be a distinction of true and false? By what is speech obscured that there should be a distinction of "is" and "is not"? How can the Tao depart and not be there? And how could there be speech and yet it be not appropriate? The Tao is hidden by petty virtues. Speech is obscured by flowery eloquence. So it is that there are

contentions between the Confucianists and Moists, each affirming what the other denies and denying what the other confirms. But if we are to decide between their several affirmations and denials, there is nothing better than to apply the light of reason.

Everything is its own "self"; everything is something else's "other." Things do not know that they are other things' "other"; they only know that they are themselves. Thus it is said that the other rises out of the self, just as the self rises out of the other. This is the theory that "self" and "other" give rise to each other. Besides, [it has been said that] where there is life there is death, and where there is death, there is life. Where there is impossibility, there is possibility, and where there is possibility, there is impossibility. It is because there is "is" that there is "is not"; it is because there is "is not" that there is "is." This being the situation, the sages do not approach things on this level, but reflect the light of nature. Thereupon, the "self" is also the "other"; the "other" is the "self." According to the "other" there is one kind of "is" and "is not." According to the "self" there is another kind of "is" and "is not." But really are there such distinctions as "self" and "other," or are there no such distinctions? When "self" and "other" lose their contrariety, there we have the very essence of the Tao. Only the essence of the Tao may occupy the center of the circle, and respond therefrom to the endless opinions from all directions. Affirmation is one of the endless opinions; denial is another. Therefore, it is said that there is nothing better than the light of reason. [Adapted][9]

This passage, as well as the whole section from which it is taken, is a criticism of the partial view of things and an admonition to take a totalistic view of it. With the substitution of some Buddhist terminology, it could easily pass for a passage from a Hua-yen text.

It is probably in Chuang-tzu's writings that the totalistic view of existence is urged strongly for the first time in Chinese literature, but we find it again in the later Neo-taoists, where it occurs in an even more pronounced way. Such a view of things runs, for instance, throughout the pages of Kuo-hsiang's writings, particularly in his well-known commentary on the *Chuang-tzu*, where two principles in particular are enunciated which will appear several centuries later in the Hua-yen system. These are the principles of the self-transformation of things and the necessary interrelationships among these same things. Thus, for instance, in commenting on the line of Chuang-tzu's text which says "Was what there was before the universe a thing?," Kuo-hsiang says,

In existence, what was prior to things? We say that *yin* and *yang* are prior to things. But the *yin* and *yang* are themselves things. What, then, is prior to the *yin* and *yang*? We say that nature (*tzu-jan*) is prior to them. But nature is simply the naturalness of things. Or we may say that the supreme Tao is prior to things. But this supreme Tao is supreme non-being (*wu*). Since it is non-being, how can it be prior? Thus, what can it be that is prior to things? And yet things are continuously being produced. This shows that things are spontaneously what they are. There is nothing which causes them to be such.[10]

The refusal of Kuo-hsiang to look for any external creative agency prior to the "ten thousand things" themselves, or to consider even a time prior to being, is a strong foreshadowing of the later Hua-yen doctrine of the self-creation and self-transformation of a universe which for all practical purposes is beginningless and endless.

Yet, while Kuo-hsiang denies a cosmologically antecedent creative agent and insists that things are mutually creative and sustaining through the dynamics of their own interrelationships, this does not mean that things exist in isolation from each other. In fact, their interrelationship is an extremely profound and intricate one, reminding us again of the cardinal tenet of Hua-yen—that while the universe is a universe of particulars with distinct qualities and functions, their existence, even their reality, lies more in their fundamental interrelationship than in their discreteness. We find a foreshadowing of this in the Kuo-hsiang commentary:

When a man is born, insignificant though he be, he has the properties that he necessarily has. However trivial though his life may be, he needs the whole universe as a condition for his existence. All things in the universe, all that exist, can not cease to exist without some effect on him. *If one factor is lacking, he might not exist.* If one principle is violated, he might not be living. [My emphasis][11]

This is a striking parallel to some of Fa-tsang's statements. The Hua-yen picture of existence presented in the Treatise (from which much of this material is drawn) is so close to Kuo-hsiang's that it would be difficult to deny strong influences. In the final pages of his Treatise, Fa-tsang illustrates the relationships pertaining between the individuals of a totality by means of the analogy of a building and a rafter, which is part of the building, and there too we notice that the total building is a necessary condition for the rafter just as much as the rafter is a condition for the building. Everything needs everything else.

Another element which found its way into the Hua-yen syncretism is the respect for, and delight in, the natural. It is a persistent trait in Taoist thought, and is nowhere as evident as in the poems and landscape paintings of the Taoists and Ch'an devotees. It is an element which is absent from Indian Buddhism, where there was, to say the least, little affection for the natural. However, the Hua-yen Buddhist world view leads directly to a new attitude toward the natural which is not only deeply respectful but imbued with a profound gratitude and even ecstatic appreciation. We need only abandon our usual partial, prejudiced point of view in order to discover that what was hitherto insignificant, mean, or loathsome has come to have significance, value, and beauty. A worn pair of straw sandals, a bamboo dipper, the water in the dipper, all these things are friends and helpers, worthy of reverence and gratitude.

Closely connected with this love of the natural world and its inhabitants was a tendency in Chinese Buddhism to interpret the Buddhist goal of enlightenment as a return to naturalness. In Taoist terms, this meant ceasing to pick and choose in the artificial, learned manner which has become our nature. By a return to the "source," which is that innate ability to respond innocently and in a childlike manner to experience, the individual transcended those maddening contraries of "is" and "is not" which Chuang-tzu spoke of, and learned the difficult art of noncalculating action, or the nonaction in action which in Chinese is called *wu-wei*. The enlightened person is presumably he who has expunged from his nature the learned responses to life's situations which lead ordinary men to favor one experience over another.[12] In "returning to the source," the individual has discovered that inmost core of subjectivity in which all the ferocious contraries are completely resolved. The difference between this view of the sage and that of Indian Buddhists can be seen quite clearly when we compare the two as portrayed in their respective traditions. The Indian figure—a Mañjuśrī, Śākyamuni, or Avalokiteśvara—is dressed in a manner befitting royalty, and royalty they are, though not a profane royalty. Jewels hang from neck, ears, arms, and legs; the hair is elaborately arranged; and he wears the robes of a prince. The pose is especially remarkable. The figure often sits cross-legged in yogic meditation, regal, aloof, with eyes half closed in eternal *samādhi*, the faint smile on the lips betraying the unspeakable bliss of one who has found a peace far removed from the dust and turmoil of the earthly arena. In contrast, the Chinese saint, perhaps best portrayed in the figures of Pu-tai and those rascally saints Shih-te and Han-shan, is frequently rather fat, jovial, and totally relaxed. He is barefooted and his hair and clothes (more like rags) are in negligent disarray. He obviously still enjoys plum wine and a good meal; there is nothing of the renunciant about him. He travels freely from village to village, dispensing goodies from his bag to the children who tease him and adore him, never for a moment losing the happy, silly grin of a man who knows who he is ("Nobody") and where he is ("Nowhere"). These figures are painted over and over by Chinese artists, and their lesson is clear. The emancipated individual is not superhuman or royal, like the Indian Buddhas and Bodhisattvas; he would never walk on water or levitate. And who wants to sit forever in yogic withdrawal when one can play games with the village urchins? They delight in the ordinary, the simple, and the humble—chopping wood and carrying water, therein lies the wonderful Way. To the person who has seen things in their true form, what can there be which is really negligible or contemptible?

These are some of the more important native Chinese influences on Hua-yen. There were others besides these, such as the tendency of Chinese like Fa-tsang to think of existence in terms of traditional patterns of thought. The *li-shih* pattern is one of these patterns of thought, but since it had particularly weighty consequences for the understanding and use of the Indian Buddhist doctrine of emptiness (*śūnyatā*), I shall reserve my comments on this pattern for a later chapter dealing with that doctrine.

However, among these influences, the most crucial insofar as Hua-yen was concerned was the strong tendency to take what has been called a totalistic view of existence, which was discussed in the first chapter. As will be shown in greater detail later, I believe that a study of Hua-yen will reveal that the whole system of thought is an elaborate reworking of the Indian concept of emptiness. In this way, it is a continuation of the Indian Buddhists' rather general concern with causation. It is evident from the alternative name which Hua-yen gave itself, the school of the "interdependent origination of the universe" (*dharma-dhātu pratītyasamutpāda*), that their primary concern was to demonstrate a universe in which the foremost fact was that of a pervasive, unfailing, vastly intricate intercausality or inter-conditionality, the implications of which are inestimable in terms of an individual's own relationship with the infinitely multitudinous "other." For the Chinese, the net result of such a philosophical effort was a view of existence which was totalistic rather than particularistic. In a particularistic view of existence, the emphasis is overwhelmingly on the discrete individual, whether a human being, a table, or an atom, and these entities, seen as being each locked up within the boundaries of its own skin, are considered by and large to be discontinuous with each other. Despite agreed continuity in such areas as genus, species, blood relationship, nationality, race, sex, and the like, it is felt that each individual is autonomous, isolated within its own skin, and is in no real way identical with, or continuous with, other individuals. A model for existence seen in this way would be a basket full of marbles. In a totalistic view of existence, on the other hand, *while the reality of individuals is admitted*, the emphasis is on the totality of being seen as necessarily composed of individuals which sustain each other in an unimaginably complex network of intercausality and interdependence. The tendency, then, is to see everything in terms of the totality of which it is a part. A good model for this view would be a living body.

This view of things, so evident in Chinese thought and art, happily coincided in many ways with a view of existence which was imported from India. The Chinese did not have to violently force Indian Buddhist doctrines into their own patterns of thought because there were from the beginning great, important areas of consensus.[13] The influence of indigenous Chinese modes of thought occurred in part in a subtle but significant change in emphasis and in part in reinterpretation of several fundamental Indian Buddhist ideas. But this will be discussed in a separate chapter.

From the standpoint of the Hua-yen school itself, the previous centuries can be seen as preparation for the final syncretic work of Fa-tsang and a few other central figures in the history of the school. The Ti-lun school contributed much in its concentration on the *Daśabhūmika Sūtra* and the very important commentary on it by Vasubandhu. Vasubandhu's insistence that each of the ten *bhūmis* was identical with the other nine, that all were empty and existed only by virtue of conditional interdependence, and that all the qualities of the ten stages were inherent in any one stage (including the Buddhahood of the final stage) was not only quite respectable *Śūnyavāda* but probably contributed as much to the creation of the independent Hua-yen school of later times as the data found in the *Gaṇḍavyūha* and other portions of the *Avataṁsaka Sūtra*. From the She-lun school the Hua-yen thinkers inherited the very important results of the work done on the *Mahāyāna-saṁgraha*, especially with regard to the material in that text dealing with the nature of Mind. In fact, the Hua-yen system seen as a species of *tathāgatagarbha* thought owes a very considerable debt not only to the work of the She-lun scholars, but to the whole tradition of study and exegesis of *tathāgata-garbha* thought which is epitomized in the highly systematic *Ta-ch'eng ch'i hsin lun (Awakening of Faith in the Mahāyāna)*, a work quoted frequently in Fa-tsang's writings. In building the architectonic grandeur of the Hua-yen system, Fa-tsang and his fellow Buddhists turned to the *Mahāyānasaṁgraha*, *Ta-ch'eng ch'i hsin lun*, and cognate texts and traditions for their ideas on the relationship of the absolute to the phenomenal, not to the *Ch'eng wei-shih lun* of the Fa-hsiang tradition of Hsüan-tsang and K'uei-chi.

Besides these major philosophical or scholastic traditions, the work of many individual scholar-monks not belonging particularly to these traditions also helped in the later formation of the Hua-yen school. All during the later part of the political division of China into North and South and into the following Sui dynasty, a number of monks continued to study the texts, think, and write. They pondered such problems as the relationship between the two spheres of the absolute and phenomenal, whether or not the absolute interpenetrated the world of desire and turmoil, and, what was particularly pertinent to later developments, whether the "ten thousand things" themselves were ultimately different, or whether in fact they might be, in some absolute sense, identical. The possibility of complete identity was offered during the Sui period by Seng-tsan, thus anticipating the work of the Hua-yen masters.[14] The point of this is that Hua-yen did not emerge full-blown with Tu-shun or any of his successors but was rather the converging point of much thought which had gone on during previous generations. Most of it was there by late Sui times (i.e., during the time of Tu-shun, the first Hua-yen patriarch) and only needed to be mastered and interrelated within a more comprehensive scheme. This work was to be accomplished by the third patriarch of Hua-yen, Fa-tsang, who, though he was presumably third spokesman for the new tradition, was in fact the real creator of what is now known as Hua-yen.

Fa-tsang's importance in the history of the Hua-yen school lay in the fact that he was more successful than any of his predecessors in effecting the great syncretizing work of his school. The foregoing discussion makes it clear that he was heavily indebted to the work of several generations of earlier Buddhists. Moreover, his own work began where the work of his immediate predecessor, Chih-yen, left off, and undoubtedly Tu-shun, the first patriarch, contributed his share to the growing tradition. However, the work of all these men was incomplete from the standpoint of the requirements of the Hua-yen school. They created pieces of the puzzle, if you will, but it was Fa-tsang, with his remarkable learning, pious zeal, and, above all, his genius for seeing relationships, who was able to take all the pieces and create a picture out of them. In essay after essay, he refined and developed the work of his predecessors, until, it is safe to say, the fully developed philosophy of Hua-yen took form in his hands. His writings, such as the Treatise, indicate that he had a very wide acquaintance with Buddhist literature, including the treatises of earlier Chinese Buddhists, and it was out of a vast knowledge which perhaps only the old Chinese scholars had at one time that he was able to create a structure which in its perfection was greater than the sum of its parts. Though his successors, Ch'eng-kuan and Tsung-mi, were able to clarify certain important facets of Fa-tsang's thought and even add a few innovations of their own, it must be said that an appraisal of Fa-tsang's work will reveal that he is the *de facto* founder and the brightest light of the Hua-yen tradition.[15]

One final point should be made concerning the Hua-yen school. It is true that for many generations of Buddhists, Hua-yen has been regarded not only as a philosophical or academic form of Buddhism but as the culmination of Buddhist philosophical effort. This is undoubtedly true, for the most part, but as was mentioned earlier, it was probably the overwhelming concern with philosophy of great difficulty that prevented the school from ever gaining a foothold among the Chinese masses. Yet it is safe to say that Hua-yen, like all forms of Buddhism, was never an end in itself. The goal of Buddhism throughout its long history has been to free men from greed, hatred, and ignorance, and whatever we may isolate from the body of Buddhism as "philosophy" or "practice" was always pursued with that goal in mind. Therefore, it may have been, and often was, good philosophy, but that philosophy existed only within the context of the Buddhist goal. This is true of Hua-yen philosophy. Fa-tsang was a great philosopher, but his philosophizing did not exist in a vacuum; it was not engaged in for the sake of intellectual fun. The Hua-yen universe as described by the philosophers was meant to be a description of existence as seen in the light of *prajñā*, i.e., as a Buddha sees it. The philosophy thus serves as a kind of road map drawn by one who has made the journey, observed the terrain, and returned. The words, admittedly a faint reflection of their referent, serve to guide and inspire us to seek the reality itself. First there is experience, then the philosophy, and either implicitly or explicitly the demand on the reader to seek the experience itself. Philosophy grows out of experience and then leads back to experience, a finger pointing to the moon of interior space. It is significant that Tu-shun, the man who is given credit for founding a school called Hua-yen, was not a philosopher at all, but rather a meditator. The only document now extant which is associated with Tu-shun, the "Practice of Tranquillity and Insight According to the Five Teachings of Buddhism," is centered around meditation; it is not a philosophical work.[16] Tu-shun *saw* in his meditations the Hua-yen cosmos which later was transformed into a philosophical system. In fact, all five Hua-yen masters wrote treatises on meditation, indicating an ongoing concern with the necessity of realizing in experience what was otherwise words on paper.[17] With Tsung-mi, who was a Ch'an master as well as a Hua-yen master, the full circle seems to be completed, for his writings show a return to a primary concern for meditation and experience. The practical implications of the Hua-yen system, as well as the background of the philosophical enterprise, are to be found in these treatises on meditation, and they indicate clearly that men like Tu-shun and Fa-tsang were not mere armchair philosophers but were aware that Buddhism is always more than philosophy; that it is, in fact, an event, a cataclysmic inner transformation without which there can be no real Buddhism at all. The Hua-yen picture of existence is grand, beautiful, and inspiring, but it is nothing if it is not a lived reality.

3

The Indian Background of Hua-yen

When Buddhologists say that Hua-yen Buddhism is the high-water mark of Buddhist philosophical development, they are referring primarily to its great concern with what we may call "causation," particularly in the form variously named dependent origination, conditioned co-production, or interdependent existence (*pratītyasamutpāda*). Undoubtedly the student of Buddhism will be impressed with the sophistication and subtlety of this concept as it has been treated by the Hua-yen thinkers. Furthermore, one wonders how this ancient concept would be capable of any greater development. To acknowledge this is to acknowledge several separate facts. First, Hua-yen is mainly concerned with causation, and we need to recall that this tradition commonly referred to itself as the tradition which taught the interdependent existence of the universe or, possibly, the interdependent existence which is the universe (Skt. *dharma-dhātu pratītyasamutpāda*). Second, what we call Hua-yen is a Chinese development of the doctrine; it arose on Chinese soil with no real counterpart in India; while men like Fa-tsang were as much Buddhists as their Indian counterparts, the perfected Hua-yen system exhibits more characteristics in common with Chinese modes of thinking than with Indian modes. This is still true despite the fact that many of the origins of the Chinese system are to be found in Indian sutras and treatises. Third, while Fa-tsang and his tradition contributed much of a distinctly Chinese character to the new tradition, its overriding concern with causation is a continuation of a strain of thought which goes back, presumably, to the earliest days of Indian Buddhism and which continued to exercise the finest minds of the sangha throughout the history of Buddhism. That is, as has already been mentioned, the problem of causation.[1] Because of this continuity, the question is now raised as to the Indian Buddhist antecedents themselves, for in order to understand just what is going on in Hua-yen thought, it is necessary to determine what the parent ideas were and what the Chinese did with these parent ideas.

We may safely say that in a sense the Chinese inherited all the concepts of Indian Buddhism. This is true in a double sense. First, although it seems that certain hallowed doctrinal items which were important to Indian Buddhists were only formally accepted by the Chinese, no teaching could really be rejected as false or unimportant, inasmuch as it was taught in the scriptures, and these were presumably an accurate recording of the true words of the Blessed One. Therefore, as Buddhists, the Chinese at least gave lip service to certain doctrinal items which in fact did not concern them greatly. An example of this is the Indian conviction that the goal is necessarily attained by a very long moral and intellectual training which precedes the goal. Second, part of the mission of the Hua-yen masters was to gather together all the important doctrines that had been encapsulated in separate traditions and recombine them into a single whole Dharma. This is a recognition of the intrinsic wholeness of the Dharma which sees that all the parts are parts of a whole. Hua-yen thus referred to itself as the "One Vehicle," *i-ch'eng* (Skt. *eka-yāna*), and the sense of the title is that there is only one path or vehicle leading to the goal, and all separate traditions or philosophical specialties are merely partial, incomplete aspects of the one whole. One vehicle universalism or catholicism thus sees the separate traditions not as competing but rather as embodying stages of development and ultimately as mutually complementary. The Dharma is one to the extent that all followers—whatever their ordination lines, whatever their philosophical specialties, whatever their sectarian inclinations—are included within the fold of the Dharma, and all will in the end find their way to Mahayana, to the whole truth, and to the final goal of Buddhahood. Inasmuch as all forms of Buddhism and all the teachings are included within Hua-yen, the latter has no teaching distinct from all other traditions, and as such it is the "one vehicle with common teaching." Consequently, Hua-yen recognizes all teachings as valid to some degree and manages to incorporate them into the body of its own system. Hua-yen thus incorporates the *dharma* theory of the Sarvāstivādins, the *anātman* doctrine, the tradition of the ten stages of the Bodhisattva's career, the doctrines of emptiness and "mind-only," the Mādhyamika dialectic, the doctrines of Buddha-nature and *tathāgata-garbha* (womb of Buddhahood), and many others.

However, while Hua-yen incorporates all these doctrines, it also has something special and distinct to offer as a tradition. It is then not only the one vehicle with common teaching, but it is also the "one vehicle with distinct teaching." In the latter capacity, it teaches something which is new in Buddhism, or which at least had existed before in only a partial, incomplete form; that is, the universe as the infinitely repeated identity and interdependence of all phenomena.

Specifically, Hua-yen teaches *shih shih wu-ai*, the interpenetration of all things, and *ch'ung ch'ung wu-chin chu pan chü-tzu. Ch'ung ch'ung wu-chin* means "infinitely repeated"; *chu* means "chief" or "primary," and *pan* is "retinue," or "secondary." If one object is analyzed in relation to all other objects, the one object is the "chief" and the others are the "retinue." But depending on point of view, any object is simultaneously both *chu* and part of *pan. Chü-tzu* means "possessing," so that the whole phrase may be translated as "the infinitely repeated possession of retinue by the chief." Thus, inasmuch as Hua-yen incorporates all Buddhist teachings, it is the one vehicle with common teachings; but inasmuch as it recombines these diverse elements into the special teaching mentioned above, which does not exist elsewhere in Buddhism and which is presumably the total truth, it is the one vehicle with distinct teachings.

If we investigate those elements which were of *primary* importance in the creation of the Hua-yen system, we find that there were two, which are in fact very closely related. They are the doctrines of emptiness (*śūnyatā*) and the "womb of Buddhahood" (*tathāgatagarbha*). We might, as a matter of fact, characterize Hua-yen as a species of *tathāgatagarbha* thought which is in turn based on the doctrine of emptiness. Even this is not the whole truth, for it tends to distort the relationship between the two doctrines. Ultimately, *śūnyatā* and *tathāgatagarbha* are alternate expressions for the same reality. Thus, according to a text cited occasionally by Fa-tsang, " '*paramartha*,' O Śāriputra, is an expression for *sattva-dhātu*; '*sattva-dhātu*,' O Śāriputra, is an expression for *tathāgatagarbha*; '*tathāgatagarbha*,' O Śāriputra, is an expression for *Dharma-kāya*."[2] That is, the realm of beings, the highest truth, and *tathāgatagarbha* are the same thing. When we speak of *śūnyatā*, we are within the realm of the epistemological and ontological. When the term *tathāgatagarbha* is used, we are concerned with this same reality but now with reference to soteriology. The former hints of the nature of truth, while the latter tells us where it is and implies a course of action.

Both doctrines played a tremendous part in the formation of Hua-yen thought, and both had had a long history in India prior to their utilization by Hua-yen. Before any discussion of the details of Hua-yen thought, we must turn briefly to the two doctrines as they were used in India and then consider the changes that occurred in them when they were used by Fa-tsang and his tradition. Little in the way of a full-length treatment has been written in a Western language on *tathāgatagarbha* thought,[3] but there are several books on the *śūnyatā* doctrine,[4] which the reader may consult for alternate interpretations or for details necessarily neglected in the following summary.

Sarvam Śūnyam

"Everything is empty." This terse but momentous statement, which is the conceptual foundation of Mahayana Buddhism, first appeared in India as the message of a group of scriptures named the "Perfection of Wisdom" (*prajñāpāramitā*). They were probably composed about 350 years after the death of the Buddha. But this was only their first appearance in literary form, and we are still unsure as to how long prior to this time the concept may have been entertained within the sangha. It must have antedated its literary debut by some time, although how long is unclear. Some Buddhologists have suggested that this concept, as well as others now identified as "Mahayana," may well have existed side by side with others considered to be more orthodox as far back as the formative days of Buddhism.[5] Thus what may seem to be a radical innovation within the Buddhist community may well have been simply the new prominence and power of a group of monks who preferred "Mahayana" ideas. In other words, the dawning of a distinct tradition called "Mahayana" may have been the emergence from relative obscurity of a doctrine which had been preferred by a segment of the sangha for several prior generations. At any rate, with the appearance of the sutras on the perfection of wisdom, the Buddhist world was transformed by a message which is stunning in its brevity and simplicity, difficult in its apprehension, and impressive in its implications for action in the world.

At a late period in the development of the *Prajñāpāramitā* literature, a synopsized version of this vast literature was composed, named the *Heart Sūtra*. It will be useful here for purposes of discussing the message of this literature because it contains, in the space of about two printed pages of English translation, the very heart or essence of the doctrine. As Edward Conze has pointed out, all this vast literature says, over and over, is "Everything is empty,"[6] and this is what we find in this synopsized version. Structurally, the sutra is a sustained criticism of the older Buddhist belief that the irreducible components of existence—*skandhas*, *āyatanas*, *dhātus*, etc.—are real, independent entities. The sutra proceeds systematically to apply the criticism of emptiness successively to the *skandhas*, *āyatanas*, and *dhātus*, saying that each is empty. Then it proceeds to such hallowed items as the Four Holy Truths, ignorance, the elimination of ignorance, and the attainment of the goal, *nirvāṇa*. All are said to be empty. Toward the conclusion of the sutra, it is said that there is nothing to be obtained, and it is because the Bodhisattva relies on the perfection of wisdom and attains this "nothing-to-be-obtained" that in the end there is final *nirvāṇa*. In a very brief space, then, the sutra has in effect claimed that all things without exception are empty, including the holy truths of Buddhism. Thus there is no thing anywhere at any time that is exempt from this emptiness. But what is emptiness? The sutra does not tell us, nor do the other Mahayana scriptures, which are notoriously silent and undemonstrative when it comes to proving, explaining, or demonstrating. Our sole clue comes from the very beginning of the sutra, where it is said that Avalokiteśvara saw five *skandhas* and perceived that they were empty of independent existence (*svabhāva-śūnyā paśyati sma*).

It was the office of the great treatise writers such as Nāgārjuna to elucidate and clarify the meaning of emptiness and to combat incorrect interpretations. The doctrine lends itself easily to wrong interpretations, and from the beginning some saw the doctrine of emptiness as a species of nihilism which would undercut religion and the ethical life. Some came to the conclusion that emptiness is the inner essence of things which could be perceived with special training. Those who saw the doctrine as a nihilistic threat interpreted the expression *sarvam śūnyam* as meaning that nothing whatever exists. The others interpreted emptiness as an entity, somehow more real than ordinary things, inhering in these things and constituting their true being.

These views are taken up by Nāgārjuna in his *Mādhyamika-kārikās*, and by Candrakīrti in the *Prasannapadā* commentary on Nāgārjuna's verses, and each view is systematically refuted. Nāgārjuna warns us (Ch. 24) that he who grasps emptiness incorrectly is destroyed, like a man who incorrectly picks up a snake. To the question of whether emptiness is equivalent to mere nonbeing, he replies, "You understand neither the object of emptiness, nor emptiness itself, nor the meaning of emptiness" (Ch. 24, vs. 7).[7] Candrakīrti adds, in his commentary, "Victim of your own thought processes, you superimpose on [the term] 'emptiness' the false interpretation of 'non-existence.'" He continues: "But in this treatise we are not giving emptiness the meaning which you are attached to."[8] He then makes the crucial point that emptiness is taught "in order to put all distinctions to rest without exception," including such distinctions as being and nonbeing.[9] Thus emptiness is not nonexistence, nor does it imply nihilism, because emptiness is a device the object of which is to criticize all views and all philosophies. In fact, even emptiness itself, inasmuch as it can become the sole remaining view when all others are destroyed, is no less exempt from the criticism of emptiness. Even emptiness is empty.

Is emptiness then some substance or essence of a metaphysical nature which remains when the yogi penetrates beneath the superficial, illusory surface of things? After all, the expression "everything is empty" seems to indicate this in attributing the predicate "emptiness" to things. When we say, "The flower is blue," we look for the blue in the flowers; when we say "everything is empty," we should look for something called "emptiness" in things. This problem has been acerbated within Buddhism itself from time to time by the tendency to hypostatize emptiness and give it a positive content.[10] Also, the emotionally warm apostrophes to emptiness in some texts might easily lead to the suspicion that emptiness is some *thing*, a spirit or entity wholly transcendent and supreme, a wholly other beyond the world of *saṁsāra*. But Buddhists have always been wary of a practice which will lead to a final attachment to emptiness, and it has been said that such an attachment is so destructive that it is better for a person to be attached to the concept of *ātman* than to that of emptiness. Emptiness is not a thing, nor is it even a superior view which is meant to replace less tenable views. Emptiness is meant to oppose all views, even the view of emptiness. It is this knowledge that even emptiness is empty that has saved it from reification and deification. Thus the negation of views and systems of thought is absolute; the *Śūnyavāda* negation does not imply an alternative "correct" position. The correct view is no view.

The suspicion that the doctrine of emptiness undercuts religion and the ethical life, as well as the value of phenomenal existence, is in turn based on the mistaken notion that emptiness is equivalent to utter nonbeing. In the *kārikās* (Ch. 24), an imaginary opponent objects that if everything is empty, then the Four Holy Truths do not exist, and consequently there is no elimination of ignorance or the attainment of the goal. Ultimately, neither do the Three Jewels exist, so that there is no Buddhism, no community of believers, and not even a Buddha. Nāgārjuna devotes most of Chapter 24 to showing that, on the contrary, if things are *not* empty, then the elimination of ignorance, the holy life, and the final goal are likewise impossible. It is rather the opponent's view of all things as having independent existence by virtue of some metaphysical substance which mitigates all moral and intellectual change either for the better or worse. Why this is so will become clearer in the succeeding discussion; indeed, the whole of the Hua-yen philosophy itself is a substantiation of this point.

These errors all arise from the misplacement of *śūnyatā*. Richard Robinson has clearly and accurately placed emptiness:

> Emptiness is not a term in the primary system referring to the world, but a term in the descriptive system (meta-system) referring to the primary

system. Thus it has no status as an entity, nor as the property of an existent nor an inexistent. If anyone considers it so, he turns the key term in the descriptive system into the root of all delusions.[11]

Elsewhere Robinson says, "Emptiness is not a term outside the expressional system, but is simply the key term within it. Those who would hypostatize emptiness are confusing the symbol system with the fact system."[12] Emptiness is not some entity "out there" in the objective world but rather a term which negates the system of words and concepts with which we categorize that which is "out there." Whenever we attempt to grasp experience through the medium of any concept, such as "existent" or "nonexistent," we are superimposing a character on the objective world which is in fact not there in the world at all; "existent" and "nonexistent" (or any other character) exist only in our minds, not "out there." Emptiness functions as a weapon which destroys the naive, uncritical belief that such concepts refer to entities. This is why emptiness as a concept must also be emptied, for inasmuch as human turmoil results from the dogmatic adherence to concepts, any concept is pernicious, including that of "all is empty." It is of no use to simply substitute one concept for another.

The problem with words and concepts is that instead of understanding that they have a purely provisional status and a purely utilitarian value, human beings tend to believe that there is a really existing entity to which the word or concept corresponds. It is the fundamental teaching of Buddhism that there is only incessant change, or flux, and that there is no thing which undergoes the change. There is a very great difference between this view and that which is commonly held; the former rests on the naive assumption that there is really an object (or complex of objects) which undergoes successive states—i.e., birth, subsistence, and cessation—but which itself is a real entity serving as the locus for the change, while the second view rests on the assumption that there is *nothing but change*, with no real, permanent locus for the change. The intricate fabric of being is thus not really being at all but a ceaseless becoming, pure flux. The change itself at any point comes about as a result of other events which act as the environment of the one point and condition it, causing it to assume a new, different, momentary form. These conditioning events themselves have no more permanence and stability than the one point mentioned above, because they in turn are being conditioned by other events. The web of interconditionality is thus nearly infinite in scope. For this reason, there is no point anywhere which is exempt from this process of change, and nothing anywhere which lasts in one form for two moments in a row. In this maze of interconditionality, to speak of real objects is a highly artificial process which is indebted to abstraction, and, according to adherents of the doctrine of emptiness, it is a futile process completely divorced from reality.

This view of existence as change by virtue of interconditionality is called *pratītyasamutpāda*, and it is, basically, a substitution for a view of real entities undergoing modification. On the one hand, such a view rejects the common-sense impression that events possess a permanent, fixed being of an autonomous nature. On the other hand, it sees "things" as being mere abstractions from the process itself, possessing a merely conventional existence the purpose of which is social and utilitarian. This does not at all deny the existence "out there" of something which I may hold in my hand or bump into in the dark. I may desire some milk and ask someone to go get the cow, and he will return with something that has horns, udder, brown-spotted skin, and that says "moo." I will thus have milk. The real issue is the *nature* of this something which I call "cow." Is its cowness something which is given by nature, or is it an abstraction superimposed on a point in space-time which is ever changing and never the same for two successive instants? The trouble with using words the way we do is that in believing that there is *really* an objective referent for the word, I can also believe that it is possible to possess it. Along with "cow" there is a whole constellation of other "real" entities, such as "me," "mine," "possessing," "good," and "bad," and it is this situation which causes human turmoil, hatred, greed, killing, envy jealousy, and so on. We cannot really possess (or lose) because there is no enduring object to possess. It is like trying to grasp a rapidly moving stream in our hands; it not only slips through our hands, we end up all wet.

But once we are able to perceive that there is change only, and that we ourselves are a part of the change, there is no longer anything to possess, no me to possess, no such thing as possession. Moreover, I can understand that the impulses which torment me and of which I am ashamed have no more solidity and fixity than any other event. If anger, for instance, were to possess any independent, real existence, then I would be faced with a great problem, for it would exist in me apart from other internal or external causes, a constant personality defect with which I would have to cope. However, since anger is a momentary state arising from conditions and then subsiding because of other conditions, when it is gone, it is really gone, extinct. I am thus not *intrinsically* an angry person, or a good person, or a bad person, or any other kind of person. The point is, I need not become obsessed with momentary states, nor need I be anxious about or ashamed of some imaginary fixed character. These momentary states thus have no hold on me at all. I am always free to assume a new state in the next instant. All events, whether psychic or material, are mere momentary links between an extinct event and a new one which does not yet exist, momentary and fleeting. "Things" are only abstractions from a process which constantly, rapidly changes simultaneously at every point, in what Whitehead called "the creative advance into novelty." Here, no self or other selves can be found to compete, hate, and destroy in what, to use another phrase of Whitehead's, is a "bagatelle of transient experience."

This "interdependent being" is a synonym for *śūnyatā*, as Nāgārjuna says in his *kārikās*, and Candrakīrti reaffirms this in commenting that "arising by conditions and emptiness are thus synonyms."[13] For something to be empty means to be empty of independent being (*svabhāva*), which is synonymous with existing only in dependence upon the other. It is because emptiness is the same as interdependent being that Nāgārjuna can say that it is just because events are empty that the religious life and its goal are possible. They are possible because of the very fluidity, the nonfixedness, of events; unwholesome states pass away into extinction, and wholesome states can arise under the influence of the proper conditions. If states such as hatred or benevolence exist in and of themselves, the individual cannot change and modification is precluded. Also, because emptiness is interdependent being, it is not tantamount to nihilism, for emptiness does not cancel out nature as a hallucination. Primarily, the doctrine of emptiness is an attack on the conceptual mode of grasping the world. It says that although words and concepts are normally valid for purposes of accomplishing our business, they are totally invalid from the standpoint of the highest truth, wherein it is seen that there is nowhere a fixed entity which corresponds to the label. It is for this reason that compassionate action in the world is possible for the Bodhisattva, for although he leads countless beings to *nirvāṇa*, according to the *Vajracchedikā Sūtra*, he does so, and can only successfully do so, as long as there exists in him no concept of beings. Any adherence to the concept "beings" would be a direct contradiction with his nature and would prevent his exercising the skillful means which become effective only with the removal of the conceptual grasp of being. Because he works in the context of complete freedom from concepts, he must, in his career, move even beyond the concept of emptiness, because this last concept freezes the fluid nature of reality no less than does the concept of selves.

It seems that the emptiness doctrine as it was held in India had mainly an epistemological force and did not assert the existence in the natural world of some metaphysical substance of a transcendental nature. However, ontology is necessarily brought into a discussion of the means and nature of knowledge, for to say that concepts do not grasp the real nature of things is to imply, however tacitly, a real nature. The Bodhisattva who has become free from concepts is presumably in contact with a reality which is obscured for most of us by the screen of words, images, symbols, and patterns of thinking. But Mahayana Buddhism in India, and primarily in its Mādhyamika form, has always been reluctant to try to say just what reality is apart from our ideas of it. We know that it is incessant change and pure fluidity, but these words themselves are understood to be only inadequate attempts to be accurate. We do not know what a Buddha sees. However, it does seem that Nāgārjuna and others in India who taught the doctrine of emptiness were primarily emphasizing a *way* of knowing, and they did not believe that emptiness was something to be observed in phenomena. If there is something which we may call the absolute, it is not some transcendental spirit or entity lurking behind the world of mere appearance, but is really the mode of apprehending the world about us; as T.R.V. Murti said, the absolute is intuition or insight itself (*prajñā*).[14] This is further substantiated by the very useful doctrine of the three natures. According to this doctrine, each thing has three natures (*trisvabhāva*): there is the nature which consists of being dependent on another, and this is the phenomenal world in its interdependent existence discussed previously in several places. Then there is the nature of being discriminated; this is the dependent nature now bifurcated into subject and object, and which is further falsely discriminated in its objective aspect. Finally there is the perfected nature, which we may also call the "absolute"; this is, according to the texts, nothing else but the dependent nature *perceived*, or *understood*, apart from the discriminated nature. The dependent nature, which is the natural world of phenomena, does not at all change itself, nor does the new dawning of *prajñā* reveal some previously obscured spirit glowing within the objects of perception. The change has taken place in the perceiver; it is his new nondual perception which is of highest value and which frees him from *saṁsāra*.

It is abundantly clear in the whole of Mahayana literature that perceiving things in the light of *prajñā*, or seeing things in the empty mode of perception, leads to a higher affirmation which is marked by clear-headed action and profound compassion. However, there also seems to be some basis for the feeling on the part of many Chinese Buddhists, as well as some Indian contemporaries of the *Śūnyavādins*, that there was something negative about the doctrine.[15] The problem originated in a simple matter of emphasis, for while emptiness and interdependent being are synonymous, the former term seems to have negative connotations lacking in the latter. Indians, whether Buddhists or otherwise, have traditionally sought the higher spiritual life through detachment from what we might simply term the "natural." Buddhist literature is well known for the abundance of passages which portray physical functions and natural objects as disgusting, and while it is true that from the standpoint of the highest truth the world is neither desirable nor loathsome, nevertheless the common strategy for emancipation was to *devaluate* these common elements of experience. "Emptiness" may be the same as "interdependent being," but to say that something is empty is to devaluate that thing, to see it as an intangible, slippery, impermanent bit of phantasmagoria not worthy of one's attention and totally incapable of supplying any lasting satisfaction. Emptiness removes it from serious consideration. The object thus becomes delusive to the meditator because in *seeming* to be something capable of being possessed or controlled, it will surely lead to frustration and sorrow when it evades the grasp. Actually, such a negation of personal value and meaning may even be inherent in the emphasis on interdependence, for Whitehead also, in reflecting upon existence as a rapidly changing stream of process in which substances were utterly lacking, ruefully reflected that life is "a flash of occasional enjoyments lighting up a mass of pain and misery, a bagatelle of transient experience."[16] At any rate, for Indian Buddhists, emptiness was a weapon which demolished ordinary value and significance in the world. Once that value and meaning was demolished thoroughly, a higher value and meaning emerged which expressed itself in the selfless career of the Bodhisattva. However, his power and effectiveness were won at the expense of those factors of experience which most ordinary men prize most. But there was a latent potential within this doctrine for a more affirmative or positive approach to emancipation which was to be exploited by the Chinese (to be discussed later).

Sarvasattvās tathāgatagarbhāḥ

"All beings are the wombs of Buddhahood." The emptiness doctrine cannot be thoroughly discussed without a brief review of another doctrine which was important in the development of Indian Buddhism and which had a great impact on Chinese Buddhist thought. This is the doctrine of *tathāgatagarbha*, "the womb of Buddhahood." This doctrine, in the words of D.S. Ruegg,

> deals essentially with the presence among all beings of a spiritual embryo or element which is basically pure and naturally luminous, whose envelope or gangue of defilements is merely extrinsic and adventitious. And by virtue of the nondifferentiation of this spiritual principle representing the absolute reality in its causal state, and in spite of the division of beings into classes which are conditionally distinct following temporarily different paths, all beings without exception thus have the certainty of attaining the state of Buddhahood—supreme, perfect awakening—and *nirvāṇa*. [My translation of the French][17]

Closely related to this doctrine is another, that of *gotra*, which means clan or lineage, and this doctrine consists of the teaching of the affiliation of all beings to either one certain lineage which will result in their attainment of Buddhahood, or to one of several lineages which direct the respective members of each lineage to a particular goal, such as Arhatship and Pratyekabuddhahood. As with the concept of *tathāgatagarbha*, there is the assertion of some element or quality possessed by each being which ensures his ultimate attainment of some spiritual fruit, often Buddhahood.

Whether the doctrine of *tathāgatagarbha* or that of *gotra*, the basic idea is that of some element which is intrinsic to beings which will ensure their ultimate attainment of the goal. The doctrine of *tathāgatagarbha* is a recognition of the fact that the goal of Buddhahood is not to be sought exterior to beings themselves, in some other time and place, but is a potential always existing within them. Thus *sarvasattvās tathāgatagarbhāḥ*, translated as "all beings are the wombs of Buddhahood," means beings are the containers or matrix in which Buddhahood can grow. Sometimes, however, a text seems to interpret the Sanskrit as meaning "all beings *possess* the embryo (or seed) of Buddhahood," in which case the emphasis is on the fact that there is a seed-potential found in beings which is the cause for the ultimate result of Buddhahood. In the first case, the emphasis is on beings as wombs or receptacles, while in the second the emphasis is on the seed-potential itself. However, needless to say, either one implies the other.

But in Indian Buddhist literature, for the most part this seed or potential is merely a seed, the undeveloped source or cause of the fully grown fruit of Buddhahood. It does not exist within ordinary beings in its fully developed state as fruit-result, and so the concept is closely bound up with the corollary concept of potential and with the defiled nature of ordinary beings. Consequently, training is necessary to mature the seed-potential. The potential, that is, must be made manifest, a concrete reality in life, and as Professor Ruegg's statement shows, the seed-potential is *merely* potential, because it is obscured by extrinsic moral and intellectual faults (*kleśa*). Once these are removed, the element itself, which is eternally pure and luminescent, shines forth in dazzling brilliance. The value of the doctrine seems thus to be twofold: it locates the goal within the seeker himself, and it indicates the necessity for purification, for the *garbha* (seed) or *dhātu* (element) must first be freed from accidental *kleśa*. In more general terms, the doctrine is soteriological in nature, and not cosmological, as it tends to be in Chinese Buddhist thought.

The Indian Buddhists, in insisting on the potential nature of the *tathāgatagarbha*, were concerned with avoiding a misapprehension concerning the nature of this element. For to concede that the *garbha* was exactly identical with Buddha-result could easily have led to the suspicion on the part of some that the doctrine of *tathāgatagarbha* was merely a Buddhist substitute for the Hindu doctrine of Brahman, in which the *ātman* of beings is identified with Brahman. This would have led to a pantheistic interpretation of *tathāgatagarbha* which would have horrified Buddhists, and at the least it would have fostered a substantialist interpretation which, along with the pantheist, would have been a betrayal of the most ancient and fundamental position of Buddhist thought. Therefore, a sharp distinction was made between cause and result, with the *garbha* or *dhātu* being interpreted as cause (*hetu*)[18] and viewed as mere potential, not at all full, perfect Buddhahood, which is the stage of result (*phala*). Even when certain texts assimilated the *tathāgatagarbha* to *tathatā* (Ultimate Reality), Buddhahood, *Tathāgata*, and *śūnyatā*, the distinction was made between this reality in its defiled state (*samalā-tathatā*) and in its purified state (*nirmalā-tathatā*). The first is none other than living beings in their ordinary state of ignorance, which is the prevailing interpretation of the term *tathāgatagarbha*, while the second is perfect Buddhahood itself.

The status of the *tathāgatagarbha* may be further clarified if it is seen in the context of the universalism of Mahayana Buddhism. In a system such as Mahayana, such a doctrine, at least in some form, is perhaps a necessary outcome of an insistence on the possibility of universal emancipation. This possibility itself is based on the recognition, taught throughout the Mahayana sutras, that the "tormentors" (*kleśa*), such as hatred or greed, are not really-existing things which infest beings and which constitute real, permanent facets of personality. Since these factors appear merely as a result of conditions, they can be removed by *anyone* who trains properly and comes to see their true nature. The doctrine of *tathāgatagarbha* is *upāya*, a means, like all other doctrines, the function of which is to express the possibility of universal perfection due to the contingent nature of the *kleśa*. In short, then, the *tathāgatagarbha*, whether container-being or contained-seed, must be seen as possibility, potential. It is the motivating source of practice because it instills confidence and assurance, for there is no one who cannot transform himself if he will but make the attempt. No one is left out; all are wombs of Buddhahood.

The doctrine of *tathāgatagarbha* is often considered to be the special possession of the Vijñānavādins or Yogacārins, for the concept of a seed potential or of a womb-like container in which Buddhahood grows is in fact often encountered in Vijñānavādin texts, such as the *Laṅkāvatāra Sūtra*, *Saṁdhinirmocana Sūtra*, and the *Mahāyānasaṁgraha*, where *tathāgatagarbha* is often assimilated to the concept of the *ālaya-vijñāna*. The *ālaya*, or "receptacle-consciousness," which is the storehouse of impressions in seed form, is in such texts conceived as the *garbha*. When the store-consciousness is purified through the "transformation of the basis" (*āśraya-parāvṛtti*) it becomes the source of Buddhahood, for it contains, from beginningless time, not only the seeds of defilement and ignorance, but the seeds of purification and wisdom as well.

However, as Professor Ruegg has argued, the doctrine does not belong exclusively, or even primarily, to the Vijñānavādins.[19] It not only does not conflict with the doctrine of emptiness but may be seen as a development within the latter doctrine, and some texts, such as the *Śrīmālādevī Sūtra*, equate *tathāgata-garbha* with *śūnyatā*.[20] The Mādhyamika treatises do not make this correlation, probably due to their concern with combating all doctrines and views, but some other *Śūnyavāda* texts less concerned with this occasionally discuss the *garbha*. The main concern of course is to avoid an interpretation of *tathāgatagarbha* as assimilated to *śūnyatā* which will make either one a positive entity of a substantial nature. But as long as these interpretations are avoided, there seems to be no objection to equating the two. As was remarked earlier in this chapter, if the term *śūnyatā* is used, the emphasis is on the epistemological and perhaps ontological; if *tathāgatagarbha* is used, the stress is on the soteriological and "practical." The doctrine of *tathāgatagarbha* stresses the innate potential for Buddhahood in beings, but this Buddhahood itself is nothing more than the perfection of the ability to experience reality in the emptiness mode, and so we may legitimately conceive of this emptiness mode of perception as an innate potential capable of develop-ment or of being freed from various obstacles. Indian Buddhist texts seem to have, for the most part, used the doctrine of emptiness when occupied with a criticism of the common mode of experiencing reality, that is, when criticizing the conceptual mode of experiencing the world. However, when addressing themselves to the question of whether this correct mode of perception was innate or acquired, they rather spoke of the seed-potential existing in beings from beginningless time. But we must remember also that the *tathāgatagarbha* refers to beings in the state of ignorance and passion, and so the doctrine of "womb of Buddhahood" is partially addressed to the problem of why beings are not able to see things as empty and why they cannot live as Buddhas.

The relationship between the two doctrines will be made clearer in a separate chapter devoted to the cosmic Buddha, Vairocana, who symbolizes this reality, but here some mention needs to be made of the Chinese utilization of the two doctrines and of their identity.

It is my contention that although Chinese Buddhists of an earlier period may have made some serious errors in understanding the doctrine of emptiness, certainly by the time of Fa-tsang the Chinese had grasped the doctrine correctly, so correctly that they were able to deal truly creatively with it.[21] The Hua-yen thinkers such as Fa-tsang discuss the doctrine essentially like the Indian masters did. The one difference, as I have already mentioned, is one of emphasis, or perhaps point of view. That is, the main difference is that the Chinese chose to emphasize the point that *emptiness is interdependence*. But interdependence is also emptiness, and even for the Chinese the fact of emptiness functioned as a way of criticizing the common mode of experience, thus devaluing it, so that this aspect was not ignored. But what is evident in the Hua-yen texts is that simultaneously as the empty mode of perception abolished the clinging to the concept of substances or selves, there emerged from the new mode of experience a very positive appreciation for the way in which things related to each other in identity and interdependence. This is what seems to be lacking in the Indian literature. The genius of the Chinese lay in their ability to interpret emptiness in a positive manner without hypostatizing emptiness, without falling into the error of even greater attachment to the world, and without abandoning the basic Buddhist conviction that ordinary experience is delusive and destructive. Thus by "positive" I do not mean that emptiness became a positive entity, which would have been extremely un-Buddhist, but that in its emphasis on interdependent being, Hua-yen was able to retain a positive, even joyous, appreciation of the absolute value of each facet of this being.

Fa-tsang himself was well aware of this difference in emphasis. In the tenth chapter of his Treatise he makes the following statement:

> The eight negations [of Nāgārjuna] are based on negation; the six meanings [of cause] are based on affirmation. In the eight negations, the principle is manifested by the negation of commonsense judgments; in the six meanings, these commonsense judgments are negated by manifesting the principle. [However,] these two [methods] are merely two sides of the same coin.[22]

By "principle," presumably "lacking in an independent being" is meant, for according to the commentary on this passage by the Japanese Kegon master Gyōnen, both Fa-tsang and Nāgārjuna accomplished the same end: both demonstrate that things do not exist independently of each other.[23] This seems to be the essence of the matter. Nāgārjuna uses the "eight noes"—no arising, no cessation, no destruction, no permanence, etc.—to demonstrate that things do not exist as substantial entities in and of themselves. However, as is well known, he avoided making any positive statement about the world in its "suchness." Fa-tsang attacks the problem from a unique angle; he shows how any object functions as an active cause in six different ways, and by stressing the active, creative force which any object exerts on all other objects, he also demonstrates that phenomena exist only in interdependence and have no self-existence. The result is substantially the same as that arrived at in Nāgārjuna's method, but the way in which the demonstration is made is very different, and the difference is significant in the way in which someone like Fa-tsang saw phenomena. He was not merely content with demolishing false views; he wished to give some idea, however imperfect, of the way things looked to a Buddha, that is, the glory and splendor of being illuminated by *prajñā*.

It seems clear from this passage from the Treatise that Fa-tsang was concerned with the traditional function of the *śūnyatā* doctrine, but as he himself says, his strategy is to demonstrate interdependent existence, or conditioned co-arising in an affirmative or positive manner, which is to show how a *dharma* is causal in six ways. Also, because the causal power is freely exerted among all phenomena, the *dharma* or object is also shown to be a result or effect of other causes. Thus the *dharma* is demonstrated to exist only due to supportive conditions and is utterly lacking in independent being. Nāgārjuna's strategy is just the reverse; the commonsense judgments of "is," "is not," "arising," "ceasing," and the like, are shown to be inappropriate, and in the course of negating all views, the principle, the nonexistence of independent being, is manifested. The difference in strategy, to repeat, is considerable. With Fa-tsang's method, there is a very strong emphasis on the positive manner in which *any dharma* acts as a necessary support for the others, the upshot of which is that *any* phenomenon must be viewed as having an absolute value in the nexus of interdependence. The view of uniformity or sameness of all things (*samatā*), which was attained in Indian Buddhism primarily by reducing all things to the common level of insignificance, is attained in Hua-yen by raising all things to the common level of supreme value. In both cases, the cause of turmoil, which is desiring and loathing, is removed.

Thus the main difference between the Indian and Chinese treatment of emptiness is one of approach, but it is one which has great consequences for the styles of the respective traditions, and a difference which in turn has major consequences with regard to practice. But other than this difference, one may search in vain in Hua-yen literature for any significant deviation from classical Śūnyavāda doctrine. (I shall reserve further comment on this for the later chapter on Vairocana, where I try to show the orthodoxy of the Hua-yen treatment of emptiness.)

One further clarification should be made before these comments on emptiness are concluded. According to Richard Robinson and other reliable students of the doctrine, the Indian Buddhists, notably in the Mādhyamika tradition, seem to have considered the doctrine to be epistemological for the most part. The sorts of statements which the Hua-yen masters make about the relationships among phenomena are lacking in the treatises of Nāgārjuna and his school.

These we may call "ontological" statements. But it would be a serious mistake to think that Fa-tsang and his tradition completely abandoned the epistemological force of the emptiness doctrine. Rather, the Hua-yen writers use the doctrine with a force both epistemological and ontological. Consequently, for Fa-tsang to say that "all is empty" is simultaneously to make a criticism of the ordinary, conceptual mode of experience and to indicate something of the nature of things seen correctly. Nāgārjuna probably would not have agreed with this approach, which is Chinese rather than Indian, but if both methods are equally effective in abolishing man's delusions, who is to say whether one is superior to the other or more correct?

The ontological force of the Hua-yen treatment of emptiness is nowhere more evident than in its insistence that this whole inconceivably vast and diverse cosmos in its utter emptiness is itself the *dharma-kāya*, the glorious body of the *Tathāgata*. In this insistence can be found the very great importance of the doctrine of *tathāgatagarbha* in Hua-yen thought. Reflected in the Hua-yen interest, also, there can be witnessed the great interest in the doctrine generally among Chinese Buddhists, perhaps due in part to indigenous conditions in China which facilitated the acceptance and development of Indian Buddhism.

Many scholars in the area of Chinese Buddhism believe that one of the main reasons why the Chinese became interested in foreign religion is that many elements of Indian Buddhism were often more or less consonant with ideas which had already had a long prehistory on Chinese soil.[24] These ideas are those which we call "Taoist," meaning the thought of Lao-tzu, Chuang-tzu, and the Neo-taoists, primarily. Although there were areas of difference or disagreement between the two systems of thought, there were undeniably other areas where the two seemed to share the same insights. It was the interpretation of the Tao, held chiefly by the group called "Neo-taoists" as the name for *the way in which things exist*, which predisposed Chinese thinkers to take a great interest in the doctrine of *tathāgatagarbha*. That is, the Neo-taoists rejected any interpretation of the Tao which would make it conceptually or ontologically separate from phenomena themselves. Accordingly, there is no longer any conception of the Tao as a cosmologically antecedent matrix from which the ten thousand things evolved, nor is there any understanding of the Tao as some sort of metaphysical substance inhering in things. Instead, the manner in which things exist singly and collectively, and the way in which they exist in harmonious interrelationship, is what is meant by "Tao." The similarity of this concept with that of emptiness is fairly obvious. To many who held this view of things, the *tathāgatagarbha* doctrine seemed very similar, and the difference between the parent Indian doctrine and the doctrine as it was enunciated by Chinese such as Fa-tsang is due in large part to the weighty influence of the Taoist concept on the Indian doctrine.

Again, a statement made by Fa-tsang seems to show the major difference between the Indian and Chinese concepts. In his lengthy commentary on the *Avataṁsaka Sūtra*, the *T'an hsüan chi*, he says that while the three vehicles (meaning mainly Indian forms of Buddhism) admit only to the existence of Buddha nature in its *causal* form in the minds of beings, Hua-yen sees them as also possessing it in the form of *result*.[25] What he means by this is that while all other forms of Buddhism admit only to the existence of some sort of seed-potential which functions as cause for the attainment of final Buddhahood, his own traditions offer the view that this intrinsic element which exists within all beings is none other than perfect Buddhahood itself. Actually, Hua-yen goes even beyond this position, holding that everything, animate and inanimate, possesses Buddha-nature. Neither is this a completely accurate statement; it is not a question of things *possessing* Buddha-nature, all things *are* Buddha-nature.

The ability of Fa-tsang to make this assertion is the result of much thought and work which had taken place in the centuries preceding his own time. One momentous landmark in the development of this concept was the composition of the *Awakening of Faith in the Mahāyāna (Ta-ch'eng ch'i hsin lun)*. It now appears to be almost completely agreed among scholars that this is not the work of the Indian Aśvaghoṣa but is an apocryphal text composed in China at a late period. The picture of reality portrayed in that work seems to be based on material deriving from several sources, such as the *Tathāgatagarbha Sūtra* and the *Rat-nagotravibhāga (Uttaratantra)*. The text is an attempt at systematizing various fragmentary ideas found in these other sources, and the resultant structure appears to have been completely satisfying to the Chinese, as can be attested by the great authority the treatise came to have in later Chinese Buddhism. The *Ch'i hsin lun* presents a picture of ultimate reality or truth, there referred to as the "One Mind," as assuming a dual form under the influence of conditions. The two forms are the One Mind as *tathatā*, or as ultimate reality in its intrinsically pure form, and as *saṁsāra*, in which the One Mind has assumed an impure form. What this means, consequently, is that beings are a mixture of truth and falsehood, an intersection of the absolute and the phenomenal. It is a remarkable document in the history of Buddhism because it claims the *tathatā*, the Absolute, can and does exist in an impure form as well as a pure form. Its implications are considerable, for it does not place *tathatā* outside the realm of the phenomenal, nor does it even make the absolute an order of being completely distinct from the phenomenal order. Whatever reality is, it is right here before our eyes, able to be seen if we can once cease to make false discriminations. Practice—meaning meditation, primarily—becomes the means of expunging the false and seeing existence as *tathatā*, the body of Truth.

The question of the relationship between the true and the false, or the pure and the impure, continued to exercise the minds of Buddhist thinkers in the years antedating the arising of the Hua-yen tradition. Particularly during the Sui dynasty, which corresponds in time to the beginning of Hua-yen activity, such men as Hui-yüan pondered the relationship between true and false, *nirvāṇa* and *saṃsāra*, Buddha and beings, and so on. In Hui-yüan's case, his interest is evident, among other places, in his commentary on the *Ch'i hsin lun*.[26] Others were also occupied with the same questions, and one stream of investigation and commentary which was later incorporated into the Hua-yen tradition was the *She lun* school, which based its work on the *Mahāyānasaṃgraha*. This whole line of questioning indicates that there was something very attractive about matters directly or indirectly concerning *tathāgatagarbha* thought for the Chinese.

Without doubt, Fa-tsang's position with regard to this doctrine owes much to the *Awakening of Faith*, as well as to some other texts which bore on the matter. Not only did he also compose a commentary on the *Awakening of Faith*,[27] but a study of his other treatises and commentaries, including the Treatise referred to so often in this book, reveals that he cited the *Awakening of Faith* many times as a corroboration of his own position. The content of the Treatise makes it clear that a great part of his own system was based on the ideas of the *Awakening of Faith*. He relied, that is, heavily on the word of that text that the world we see about us is a mixture of the absolute and phenomenal, and his doctrine of the identity of all things derives from his observation that if all things are both phenomenal and absolute, then despite the differences in characteristics and functions of the infinity of things which constitute the world, they are ultimately identical in sharing as their basic reality the absolute. The Hua-yen pattern of evolution whereby the immutable absolute comes to assume the form of the conditioned world of phenomena while still somehow retaining its immutability is very similar to that of the *Awakening of Faith*, though demonstrations are lacking in that rather dogmatic composition.

While relying heavily on the basic structures of the *Awakening of Faith*, Fa-tsang nevertheless took these ideas further than they had been in that text. That text, as well as his other sources, stopped with what Fa-tsang called the "identity of the phenomenal and absolute," but the *tathāgatagarbha* doctrine which we encounter in Hua-yen is unique in its picture of a conjunctively whole universe correctly seen as the mutual identity and interdependence of all the disjunctively separate objects which constitute it, this totality being none other than the One Mind and the body of the Buddha. This is the identity of phenomenon with phenomenon, a doctrine missing in the *Awakening of Faith* and other sources. Hua-yen also refers to this situation as the "*Dharma-dhātu* Buddha."[28] This Buddha which is the *dharma-dhātu* is totally present in not only human beings but in ants, grass, and dirt.

In its eclecticism, Hua-yen of course incorporates all varieties of the doctrine of reality as "mind-only," or "one mind," but the special type which is the contribution of Hua-yen may be seen in the comments which Fa-tsang makes with regard to these various types. In his *T'an hsüan chi*, he lists ten varieties of one mind or mind-only doctrine as they are presumably held by different segments of the sangha:

1. Both visual perception and its objects exist.
2. Characteristics of perceived objects are functions of perception.
3. Discrimination is a function of consciousness.
4. The derivative is a function of the fundamental (mind).
5. Characteristics (*hsiang*) are ultimately essence (*hsing*).
6. Things are formed from the transformation of Reality.
7. The phenomenal and absolute are interfused.
8. The things of the phenomenal world all interpenetrate.
9. All things are identical.
10. Characteristics and functions of all things freely interpenetrate as seen in the image of the net of Indra.[29]

These ten varieties of mind-only doctrine include the common varieties of Mahayana and non-Mahayana Buddhism. They include "Hīnayāna" (1), which is not a doctrine of mind-only at all; the doctrine held by Hsüan-tsang's Wei-shih school (2 and perhaps 3); and the doctrine of the *Awakening of Faith* (6 and 7). While these are all incorporated to some extent in the Hua-yen system, it is only the last three which are considered to be the special province of Hua-yen. That is, these last three kinds refer to the *dharma-dhātu* which is mind-only, or the one mind, as the mutual identity and interdependence of all phenomena. It is this reality which is *dharma-kāya*, and it is *tathāgatagarbha* to the extent that all phenomena without exception participate in this fundamental reality.[30]

This species of *tathāgatagarbha* seems to be more cosmological in nature than the Indian varieties in its systematic attempt to identify ultimate reality with the universe itself in its true state. Indian texts did this also, in the sense that they equated *nirvāṇa* and *saṃsāra*, as well as all other dualities, but only in the sense that all dualities were identical in their common emptiness. There seems to be at least very little concern in Indian texts with identifying the empty universe with the body of the *Tathāgata.* I say "little" because Indian texts are not completely void of statements that seem to identify the two. It is significant that many of the texts which Fa-tsang cites to substantiate his own position are Indian in origin and do contain passages which could easily be interpreted as holding an analogous position. Among these texts are such sutras as the *Laṅkāvatāra, Śrīmā-lādevī,* and *Anūnatvāpūrṇatva-nirdeśa* and such treatises as the *Mahāyānasaṁgraha* and *Uttaratantra.* Thus he quotes the *Śrīmālādevī Sūtra* as saying, " 'Not impure yet impure' means that the eternal becomes the non-eternal. 'Impure yet not impure' means that when it becomes non-eternal, it does not lose its eternality."[31] Fa-tsang cites this text as substantiation for the idea that the impermanent world of things and the eternal reality are one and the same. According to the *Anūnat-vāpūrṇatva-nirdeśa,* "The *Dharma-kāya* transmigrating in the five paths [of sentient existence] is called 'beings.'"[32] From the *Mahāyānasaṁgraha* he takes another passage which apparently substantiates his claim that the absolute and conditioned are one and the same:

> There are three kinds of *dharmas* taught by the Buddha: a soiled aspect, a pure aspect, and an aspect which is both soiled and pure. Why are three aspects taught? Within the dependent nature [*paratantra-svabhāva*] the discriminated nature [*parikalpita svabhāva*] is the soiled aspect, and the nature which is *tathatā* [i.e., =*pariniṣpanna-svabhāva*] is the pure aspect. The dependent nature itself is the aspect which is both soiled and pure.[33]

Thus the phenomenal world of interdependence is capable of being seen as impure when under the hypnotic spell of discrimination or as pure when seen in the light of *prajñā.* But to see it as pure, which means to see it in its real aspect, is merely to see it as the interdependence and identity of its parts. In this way, Fa-tsang gave an authoritative basis for his own system by appealing to un-impeachable sources. However, those texts, as I have already pointed out, substantiate the view of the identity of the noumenal and phenomenal; the final step in the Hua-yen system is to assert the identity and interdependence of the parts of the whole, and it is this universe which is seen as the very body of the Buddha. It is no less empty than the universe as seen by Indian Buddhists, but there is an affirmation of it which seems to be missing in Indian Buddhism.

This view of existence is probably rightly seen as a modification of classical Indian views concerning *tathāgatagarbha.* I suspect that it was the Taoist—particularly Neo-taoist—tendency to find ultimate good in the harmonious co-existence of the phenomena of the world which led later Buddhists such as Fa-tsang to also see the ultimate good—emptiness, the body of the Buddha, reality, Buddha nature, etc.—as coterminous with a universe where ultimately all distinctions are harmonized, and in which all things are necessary conditions for the whole. It was fortunate for men like Fa-tsang that their private intuitions with regard to the structure of reality could be satisfactorily expressed in orthodox Buddhist language, and that there were indeed many doctrines within Buddhism which, properly syncretized in the subtle mind of someone such as Fa-tsang, could form a system of thought which was quite respectably Buddhist and yet conformed to a sensibility which was probably much more Chinese than Indian. Yet the intuitions which lay at the root of the Hua-yen cosmology are certainly not exclusively Chinese. After all, the figure of Vairocana, the cosmic Buddha, is of Indian, not Chinese, origin, and the figure of Dorje Sempa in Tibetan Buddhism attests to the fact that others besides the Chinese were inclined to identify the cosmos in its true nature with the body of the Buddha. What distinguishes Hua-yen and makes it unique as a system of thought is the centrality of this vision of the interpenetration in identity and interdependence of things as the supreme good, the very body of the *Tathāgata*.

In other words, we may say that the unique contribution of Hua-yen lay in its systematic attempt to syncretize various Buddhist doctrines, primarily those of emptiness and *tathāgatagarbha*, in order to give a rational basis for an intuition of the nature of things which, although foreshadowed in Indian literature, was particularly congenial to the Chinese sensibility. There is nothing mean or inferior, or anything to be despised in the whole of existence, when it is properly seen apart from self-interest. Every item in the cosmic inventory is of supreme value, for everything is empty, and therefore it contains and teaches that reality which shines from its heart.

4

Identity

The preceding chapters illustrate that the uniqueness of Hua-yen lies in its portrayal of a universe in which the distinct things that constitute it are fundamentally identical and exist only through a complex web of interdependency. It was the mission of Fa-tsang and his line to construct a rational basis for this view, which in the final analysis is an intuition growing out of meditative practices. The core of Fa-tsang's Treatise consists of a sustained, systematic attempt to demonstrate why and how things interpenetrate in this manner. The following three chapters will be devoted to a discussion of his arguments. The present chapter concerns the matter of identity, but before Fa-tsang's arguments in favor of the identity of things are discussed, there must be some analysis of a preliminary phase in his discussion, the identity of phenomena with the absolute. Chapter 5 is devoted to interdependence, and Chapter 6 demonstrates the total relationship between the one and the many, using Fa-tsang's analogy of a building.

The first step in the argument, showing the identity of the phenomenal and absolute—or *shih* and *li*, to use Fa-tsang's usual terminology—is a necessary step in the construction of the system, and it shows how certain common doctrines of Buddhism were used as "bricks" to construct the system. While Fa-tsang makes free and extensive use of almost all the common doctrines of Buddhism in order to build up his philosophy, his method is also interesting in the rather free and innovative way he uses them. Three important doctrines or devices are used in this first phase of the system: there is a basic and extensive use of the doctrine of *pratītyasamutpāda*, which is indeed the foundation of the system, this in turn is discussed within the framework of the doctrine of the three natures (*trisvabhāva*), and the proper way of viewing the three natures is discussed by means of the application of the Mādhyamika tetralemma.

The framework for this phase of the system is the doctrine of the three natures. I call it a framework because study indicates that the three natures are not themselves intrinsic to what Fa-tsang was attempting to do. The fact that he did use this doctrine seems to be due to considerations other than necessity; he might easily have used another framework with no loss to his own system.

It will be recalled that the three natures are the dependent nature (*paratantra-svabhāva*), the discriminated nature (*parikalpita-svabhāva*), and the perfected nature (*pariniṣpanna-svabhāva*). In Fa-tsang's system, the dependent nature is the nature that an object possesses consisting of its existence in total dependence on exterior conditions. The discriminated nature of the same thing consists of the *way* in which it appears erroneously to the human mind as distinct from the subject and as further endowed with a real self-existence. The perfected nature is the real nature of this object as it is apart from our suppositions. We may say that this is its suchness (*tathatā*), divorced from concepts superimposed on it because of our naive belief that words have real referents. All three natures belong to any given thing, and a common interpretation of the doctrine is that if the discriminated nature is expunged from the dependent nature, the dependent nature perceived in its real state is itself its perfected nature.[1]

This doctrine seems to have been very useful to those Buddhist academic traditions which were primarily occupied with problems of a psychological or epistemological nature, for its value lies in its ability to give some indication as to the nature of delusion and at the same time to show the nature of *prajñā*-insight. It is important psychologically because it explains the nature of the tricks the human mind plays on itself, and it is important in terms of epistemology because it casts great doubt on the ability of ordinary modes of perception to divulge reality. The dependent nature is truly pivotal in this doctrine, whether the three natures are discussed in terms of seed impressions stored in the mind or whether they are discussed, as Fa-tsang discusses them, in terms of the phenomenal world, for the dependent nature is the raw, indeterminate stuff which we humans may, and do, interpret as either *saṃsāra* or *nirvāṇa*. Thus in our stupidity and desire we may see this bare facticity of things under the sway of discrimination, in which case the dependent nature is seen as the realm of struggle and death, or we may see this same neutral stuff illuminated by the clarity of *prajñā*, in which case we see it as *nirvāṇa*.

The three natures are three distinct aspects of an object, and the three are usually not confused or identified. There are three because there is a strict antithesis between the discriminated nature and the perfected nature, and the dependent nature is in itself neither; it is just what it is, and nothing else. Furthermore, the three are distinct because they are fundamentally different in their own modes of being. *Parikalpita* does not really exist and is impermanent; *paratantra* exists but is impermanent; and *pariniṣpanna* both exists and is permanent. Basically, however, any tendency to erase the differences in the three natures would destroy their function as it existed historically in the traditions outside Hua-yen; that is, it served to indicate something of the nature of ignorance and enlightenment, and it both indicated the process whereby beings became deluded and pointed out the path to light and clarity of vision.

The above discussion of the historical function of the three natures doctrine has been made, with some simplification, from the standpoint of Hsüan-tsang's Wei-shih tradition, which was a new and influential form of Buddhism with strong imperial support during the formative years of the Hua-yen school. In incorporating it within his own system and using it in the unorthodox manner he did, Fa-tsang was trying to do at least two things. First, because it was a very important doctrine in Buddhism and because he was consciously attempting a grand syncretism of Buddhist thought, he probably felt that he had to account for it in his own system. Second, in using it in the peculiar way he did and in subordinating it to the whole of his own thought, he in effect criticized it as a merely partial form of the whole truth. A third reason may be offered: it has been suggested by some Japanese scholars that in incorporating Hsüan-tsang's doctrines into his own and subordinating them to a presumably more comprehensive, accurate world-view, Fa-tsang was hoping to decrease the amount of influence Hsüan-tsang and his school had with the imperial court and win the important royal patronage needed by an academic tradition of this type.[2] Fa-tsang could hope to do so because in many ways his Hua-yen world view supplied an interesting philosophical rationale for the relationship of the emperor (or empress) and the satellite countries coming under the rule of the T'ang court. It did in fact have such an appeal, and the Empress Wu switched her patronage from Hsüan-tsang's school to that of Fa-tsang.

Fa-tsang's strategy in laying a foundation for the idea of the identity of things is to show that, contrary to the views of the Wei-shih tradition, what we may call the true and false are not at all absolutely distinct orders of truth but are rather imbedded in each other inseparably. There is, in fact, only one reality, which is itself a mixture of the true and false. Drawing copiously on a vast amount of very respectable Buddhist literature, Fa-tsang proceeds to document a case for the existence in each of the three natures of both the true and the false. The result of this enterprise shows better than anything else what his intentions were, for in his hands the three natures become just two natures, the true and the false, or emptiness and existence. Both explicitly and implicitly, he continues the Buddhist preoccupation with the mechanisms of delusion and enlightenment, as Hsüan-tsang had in utilizing the three natures doctrine, but in effect, by reducing the three to two, he has switched the context of the doctrine, for he uses this method to show that the material world "out there" is not merely a material world, but is also the very body of the Buddha, the face of truth.

Fa-tsang's treatment of the three natures is rather ingenious, and a brief look at his procedure will help in understanding his discussion of identity. First, he names the two aspects of each of the three natures:

> [499a] The two aspects of *tathatā* [i.e., *pariniṣpanna svabhāva*] are 1. it is immutable, 2. it obeys conditions; the two aspects of the dependent nature are 1. it exists in a manner similar to the real, 2. it is without an essence of its own; the two aspects of the discriminated nature are 1. it exists to the senses, 2. it does not exist in reality.[3]

The immutability of the perfected nature consists of its ability to remain purely itself, the absolute, despite the fact that it appears to us as conditioned phenomena. On the other hand, the second aspect seems to contradict the first, for now Fa-tsang says that this same immutable absolute becomes conditioned, and this means that it takes on the form of pure and impure *dharmas*. Next, when the dependent nature is examined, it too is seen as possessing two aspects. "Existing in a manner similar to the real" means that it has a quasi-permanence and reality which make it seem to be ultimate. The second aspect contradicts this in pointing out that it has no essence or self-existence; it is indeed empty, as is anything which is produced from conditions. Finally, the discriminated nature has the aspect of existing to the senses, which means that we certainly do believe that phenomena are what they seem to be. However, the second aspect corrects this, saying that it does not really exist as it appears.

Now, if we examine these three natures in their dual aspects, it will be noticed that despite real psychological, epistemological, and soteriological differences of a crucial kind between truth and falsity, that is, between the perfected nature on the one hand and the other two natures on the other, the three natures are ultimately identical in being mixtures of the true and false. This will become evident if the three natures with their respective dual aspects are listed in a table:

	A	B
Pariniṣpanna	immutable	conditioned
Paratantra	essenceless	seems to be real
Parikalpita	nonexistent in reality	exists to the senses

Fa-tsang interprets all the qualities in row *A* as being the same. That is, the essencelessness of the dependent nature is what is called immutability and nonexistence in reality in the perfected nature and discriminated natures respectively. Fa-tsang equates all three with the true and furthermore identifies them as emptiness. Also, all the qualities under *B* are the same, and these are equated with the false and with existence, the latter being used as an equivalent to the *rūpa* of the *Prajñāpāramitā* literature. Consequently, each of the three natures shares the dual character of truth and falsity, or emptiness and existence. If conditioned being and its illusory appearance are nothing but the immutable absolute under the sway of conditions, which is what the conditioned aspect of *pariniṣpanna* means, then the absolute separation of the three natures has been destroyed, and what remains is a phenomenal world which conceals within it the eternal, immutable truth. Yet Fa-tsang was an orthodox Buddhist, and he retained the distinction between the true and the false, as indeed he had to if his philosophy was to remain consonant with the most ancient religious objective of Buddhism. Simply put, it makes a great difference to us whether we perceive only distinctions and competition or sameness and harmony; although we recognize that reality is a mixture of truth and falsity, there is a difference between the two categories. The former, which Fa-tsang in characteristic Chinese fashion calls the "root," nevertheless is the source of the "limbs" or "derivative," and the latter in turn are developments of the "root." Thus, says Fa-tsang, "The true embraces the false and derivative, and the false penetrates the true source."[4] If this seems to be a radically Chinese interpretation of Buddhist ideas, it should be remembered that we are simply involved with an unusual manner of demonstrating something which is reiterated at great length in Mahayana sutras, which is that form and emptiness are identical. The two are inseparable, because emptiness is form's mode of being, but it matters whether we perceive just form or empty form.

Fa-tsang was a very learned man, and he was able to reach deeply into Buddhist literature for passages which substantiate his vision, and it is indeed a remarkable vision. In his treatment of the discriminated nature, he merely rephrased much that had been said about it in *Vijñānavāda* texts. They too acknowledged the obvious fact that the subject–object split seems to be real enough to us, and that we really do perceive the distinctions which constitute our reality. And they were equally insistent that it was all nonexistent, pure illusion. The two aspects of the dependent nature seem to reflect Fa-tsang's knowledge of Mādhyamika views.[5] They, before Fa-tsang, spoke of the emptiness of phenomena, while at the same time admitting that the seemingly ultimate reality of these things derives from their having sprung into existence as a result of conditions. The perfected nature, however, is treated in the most unusual manner. Fa-tsang obviously made great efforts to find textual authorities to back him up, for while all schools of Buddhism agreed that *nirvāṇa*, emptiness, Buddha nature, and so on, were immutable by definition, the conditionality of this absolute was not part of orthodox Buddhist thinking. Fa-tsang's position is that this absolute comes to exist in both a pure and impure form as conditioned phenomena, and Buddhists traditionally were not inclined to agree that the Buddha-nature had a soiled aspect. For Fa-tsang to treat the perfected nature in this manner depends, perhaps, on his willingness to take liberties with the passages from older texts which leaned in that direction. In fact, the most important source for proof of his position seems to have been the *Awakening of Faith in the Mahāyāna*, which is now generally accepted as a Chinese synthesis of several other texts, perhaps given a particularly Chinese interpretation. As I mentioned in Chapter 3, the picture of the immutable absolute becoming conditioned and assuming the form of pure and impure *dharmas* follows the outline in that text, where the One Mind is said to assume a form which is a mixture of the pure and impure.

It appears that Fa-tsang had at least one precedent for asserting a dual aspect for each of the three natures. The *Trisvabhāva-nirdeśa*, for instance, speaks in the following manner of the three natures (numbers refer to verses in that text):

10. The profundity of the three natures consists of being and nonbeing, duality and unity, obscurity and purification, and nondistinction of marks.
11. *Parikalpita* is grasped as existing but does not really exist; thus it is held that its marks are both being and nonbeing.
12. *Paratantra* exists in an illusory manner but does not exist in the manner in which it appears; thus it is held. . . .
13. *Pariniṣpanna* exists in nonduality and is the absence of duality; thus it is held. . . .[6]

The verses then continue to explain how each of the three natures is also dual from the standpoint of obscurity and purification, and so on. While Fa-tsang's treatment frequently differs in particulars, and certainly in intent, the *style* of treatment is no different from that of the *Nirdeśa*. In fact, some later verses speak of the identity of each of the three natures with the other two.[7]

The main support for Fa-tsang's view of the identity of the three natures is scriptural testimony, as was mentioned above. I have quoted several illustrative passages in the section on the doctrine of *tathāgatagarbha* in Chapter 3. By ranging over an extensive collection of sutra and treatise literature, and extracting such passages as the one which says that the *Tathāgata* transmigrating in the six paths of sentient existence is called "living beings," Fa-tsang was able to make a convincing argument for the qualities he assigned to the three natures. It is evident, then, that he was mainly concerned with giving the weight of traditional authority to a view of existence as being a mixture of the true and false, or emptiness and phenomenality. The result, in Buddhist terms, is a vision of the *dharma-dhātu* as Buddha-body, *dharma-dhātu kāya*.

Finally, Fa-tsang takes great pains to forestall any attachment to the categories he has established, particularly as it might arise from a naive, crude interpretation of such categories as being and nonbeing. To do this, he subjects his own categories to a lengthy criticism through the use of the Mādhyamika tetralemma. Thus he asks, "Does the perfected nature exist?" The answer is "no," because it obeys conditions. Is it nonexistent? It is not nonexistent because it is immutable. Is it both existent and nonexistent? No, because it does not have a dual nature. Then is it neither existent nor nonexistent? No, because it is endowed with qualities as countless as the sands in the Ganges River. Then the same questions are raised with regard to the other two natures, and each is answered in the same manner. The reason this process is followed is that if the questioner thinks that the perfected nature exists in the ordinary sense of "existence," the answer must be in the negative. This attachment to a false existence is annihilationism because in asserting a misconceived existence, true existence is destroyed. The same is so for nonexistence. If *tathatā* is nonexistent, then there is no support for *dharmas*, and to assert the existence of *dharmas* without a cause is eternalism. Moreover, if it does not exist, there is no cause for holy wisdom, for (as was noted in the chapter on *tathāgatagarbha*) the cause of wisdom is innate Buddha-wisdom as *tathatā*. By means of a lengthy criticism of such views, Fa-tsang warns the careless reader not to misunderstand the language he uses when discussing the three natures.

With the attempt to cut off attachment, the first phase in the establishment of the relationship of identity is completed. By finding the two aspects of existence and emptiness within each of the three natures, he has established the identity of the three natures. However, the final result is a view of existence as a mixture of the true and false, i.e., as phenomena, but also as the absolute truth. As Fa-tsang says in conclusion to this part of his essay, the true is included in the false derivative so that there is nothing which is not the true, and the false permeates the true source so that there is none which is not included in the true. They embrace one another freely, without obstacle.

The next step in the system is basically very simple, but the validity of Fa-tsang's claim that any object, or *dharma*, is identical with all other *dharmas* depends very much on our ability to accept certain premises. First, we must accept the basic concept of emptiness itself. Second, we must be able to consider emptiness to be so completely fundamental to the being of things that despite their obvious and real differences, they are alike in a more essential way in being empty. If we can accept these premises, then the claim that all things are identical does not seem quite so improbable, because identity is claimed on the basis of this common emptiness. It is not as if Fa-tsang, or any other Buddhist, has high-handedly obliterated the differences, for the Hua-yen position is that of identity in difference. In the analogy of the body (in Chapter 1), there is no real contradiction between identity and difference; indeed, things are identical because they are different. This is neither mysticism nor badly confused thinking, which is evident once we become aware of Fa-tsang's criterion for identity.

This position of identity in difference is reflected in the analysis of a phenomenal object into two different "essences," which Fa-tsang calls "identical essence" and "different essence."[8] These two essences are derived from the unusual analysis of the three natures discussed earlier. There, Fa-tsang treated each of the three natures in such a way that each separately and all three collectively were seen to have two natures, which Fa-tsang calls, variously, emptiness and existence, the true and false, and so on. Now, when Fa-tsang speaks of identical essence and different essence, he is once again concerned with the situation whereby a *dharma* is said to be *existent* because it is solely a product of contributory conditions, and *empty* because that which comes into being as a result of conditions has no self-existence. Identical essence thus means that all things have an identical essence because all are intrinsically empty, and all have different essences because, as existents, each is different in nature. Thus fire and ice can be said to be identical because both are empty, i.e., both are products of conditions and have no self-existence. At the same time, they are different, for obvious reasons. However, the real differences between things are more pertinent to the matter of inter-dependence, as will be discussed in Chapter 5. Identity is related to the fact that all things are empty, and this relationship will be discussed in the remainder of this chapter.

When *dharmas* are said to possess an identical essence, this should not be confused with the mutual identity among *dharmas* as entities. Identical essence refers to the fact that all *dharmas* function identically as causes. This means that any *dharma* in and of itself, without any reference to another *dharma*, functions as the total cause for the totality of *dharmas*. Since the totality *as that totality* is impossible without the contributory function of this one *dharma*, and since any *dharma* functions identically in this manner, any one *dharma* is said to have a causal essence identical with all other causes. Fa-tsang derives the concept of identical essence from the ability of the one *dharma* to act in a total causal capacity without the aid of collaborating conditions.[9] A commentary on Fa-tsang's text discusses this point in the following manner:

> Because of the concept of not requiring conditions there is the category of identical essence. This means a single cause universally serves as many

conditions, so that there are many individual causes within the one cause. These many other causes and the one original cause are not differentiated, so this is called "identical essence."[10]

If this principle is then applied to some situation such as the twelve-linked chain of interdependent being, then any one link among the twelve conditions will be seen as having the same causal essence as the remaining eleven, in spite of the fact that from another point of view, ignorance and karmic preconditions, for instance, are different in other ways. What this is, then, is a recognition of the power of any one *dharma* to function as total cause, aside from any consideration of being assisted by other *dharmas*, and even aside from any question of relationship. The one *dharma* as contributory cause is no different from any other *dharma*-cause, and therefore all are identical as causes. With regard to the twelve-linked chain of interdependent being, all twelve *dharmas* are then considered to be *avidyā* from the standpoint of *avidyā* itself. If we switch our attention to another *dharma*, such as *vijñāna*, then it can be said that there are twelve *vijñānas* there. Identical essence, then, is discussed with reference to the identity of all *dharmas* in their causal capacities. There is absolutely no difference in things as far as their respective abilities to function as sole cause for the result is concerned.

Now, when we speak of the identity of things *as things*, we are speaking within the frame of reference of the simultaneous emptiness and existence of a *dharma* which Fa-tsang postulates on the basis of his treatment of the three natures. Existence means that the object exists as a result of conditions; emptiness refers to the fact that what exists in dependence on conditions has no ultimate being in and of itself. Now, if we examine the relationship between a single *dharma* conceived as a cause and the many other *dharmas* which are the result of that other cause, we will discover that despite the real numerical distinctness of the many, and despite the obvious differences in character, there is no essential difference between the one *dharma* and the many others. In short, there is a fundamental identity among all things as things.

Fa-tsang uses the analogy of ten coins to demonstrate this relationship.[11] The ten coins are an analogy for the totality of existence, and the relationship between any one coin and the remaining coins is a model for the relationship between any thing and the infinity of all other objects which constitute existence. If we start with coin one and analyze its relationship to the other nine coins singly and collectively, it will then be said that coin one is identical with coin two, coin three, all the way up to coin ten. Now the question is why. According to the reasoning of the Hua-yen masters, coin two is not a self-existent entity in its context of the ten (whole). It is coin two as a result of coin one, and looked at from the standpoint of coin one, coin one is the cause and coin two is the result, i.e., it is a conditioned coin two. If this were not the case, then even in the absence of coin one, coin two would be number two. In Buddhist terminology, it would have a self-existence. But it does not. Looked at from the standpoint of the first coin, which is an entity with a distinct appearance and individual nature, coin two, which becomes what it is purely due to the presence and conditioning function of the first coin, is empty. Consequently, coin one *exists*—i.e., is a phenomenal object—and coin two is *empty*—i.e., exists only in a conditioned manner. Next, the same may be said with regard to coin three, seen from the standpoint of the first coin. The same relationship of cause and effect and the same status of existence and emptiness pertains between coin one and each of the remaining coins.

But this is still not identity, since coin one is the cause and the other nine coins are the result, and coin one exists while the other nine are empty. Identity can be seen when it is recalled that *no* thing enjoys an independent existence, for everything enjoys a merely conditioned existence and is consequently empty. This is true of coin one, which we are in danger of thinking of as ultimately existent in contrast to its empty result. It too is empty, for it is coin one only in the context of the totality. In other words, it is conditioned by coin ten, coin nine, all the way down to coin two. Thus the remaining nine coins are now *existent* entities which function as the cause for coin one, which is the result, and as a product of conditions is *empty*. Then when we ask where the identity comes in, if we look at the relationship of coins one and two, it can be seen that coin one is existent in its emptiness (i.e., is a cause) while coin two is empty in its existence (i.e., is conditioned and is the result), but since the law of interdependent being is universal, then since coin one derives its being from the conditioning power of coin two (as well as from all the other coins), coin two is simultaneously existent in its emptiness while coin one is empty in its existence. The coins are identical in their simultaneous possession of the natures of emptiness and existence. Needless to say, the same situation exists for each of the ten coins simultaneously with respect to the remaining coins. This must necessarily be the case because causality is not unidirectional, for since *each* exerts total causal power with relation to the many, each coin must be simultaneously the cause and the caused, existent and empty. Existence is interdependent existence because this causal efficacy is exerted universally, simultaneously, and reciprocally among all *dharmas*.

The emptiness and existence which serve as the source for the identity of things function primarily as a means of indicating the flow of causal efficacy between a *dharma* considered to be cause and the totality of remaining *dharmas* which are in this context considered to be result. As I have shown, in an examination of the relationship existing between two *dharmas*, it is clear that this one *dharma* is also empty when seen as the result of another *dharma*, because causality is constant and multidirectional among all *dharmas*. Therefore, of course, any *dharma* is always both existent and empty. The reason for insisting on the existence of the *dharma* which is being considered as cause is partly to emphasize the concrete reality of the *dharma* but also, and primarily, to emphasize the conditioned, empty nature of its result. Thus Fa-tsang tends to equate the causal *dharma* with existence and the result with emptiness. But the true state of things becomes evident only when it is realized that that first *dharma*, considered to be cause, is also empty, because it is the result of other conditions at the same time it is a cause for those very *dharmas*. A good example of this may be witnessed in Chapter 6, in the causal relationship between a rafter and the barn of which it is a part.

Fa-tsang thus has a criterion for his assertion of universal identity, and the only obstacle lying in the way of admitting this identity is that of recognizing the reality of emptiness as a sufficiently important aspect of things. If it is not a sufficiently unifying quality of things, then identity becomes difficult to perceive. Hence in human affairs, the notion that all humans are "children of God" is sufficient for the perception of identity, and such a perception ideally entails a loving, humane relationship with one's neighbors, whoever they are. However, the fact that all human beings have two legs is not normally considered to be a reason for asserting identity, for although both our bipededness and our being children of God are presumably realities, one is important enough for us to postulate identity on its basis while the other remains nonfunctional. Buddhists have believed that the category of emptiness not only is more significant than that of humanity, two-footedness, and so on, but is the most significant of all, because only in the perception of emptiness are we able to become truly free of the hallucinations and nightmares that torment us. Indeed, other perceptions of the type mentioned above seem to have the contrary effect of dividing us from everything else, enslaving us to egotism, pride, hatred, and delusion.

The perception of identity is the perception of interdependence. It is the perception of the contingency and fragility of our own life, as well as that of all other things. In the perception of emptiness, we discover that we owe our being to countless other beings, animate and inanimate, near and far. From this new sense of mutual need is born a gratitude and respect which is unconditional and unqualified. The Pure Land of Amida is nothing more than this ordinary world, completely pervaded with unconditional respect and gratitude.

5

Intercausality

The single *dharma* which was examined in the preceding chapter by means of the analogy of ten coins is not completely autonomous in its ability to create the result. Looked at in isolation, purely from the standpoint of its own causal efficacy, it is true that it has the total power to create the result. What is meant by this is indicated by Fa-tsang's statement to the effect that the result is not able to be formed in the absence of the single *dharma*. Since all *dharmas* share the same power, they are said to be identical in essence. In looking at them in this manner, there is no question of the uniqueness and particularity of the *dharma*; it is, so to speak, a faceless center of causal efficacy. But this is not the whole truth. The *dharma* is an individual in the strict sense; it is unique, possessing a form not exactly like any other form, and it also has a function which is different from the functions of other, dissimilar individuals. As an individual, it thus necessarily interacts dynamically with other individuals. Now there is a recognition of the pure facticity of the individual, and consequently a recognition of its dynamic nature. A commentary on Fa-tsang's Treatise says,

> Different essence is the topic of the mutual difference of [*dharmas* of] conditioned arising. This means that within the inexhaustibly great [network of] conditioned arising, all conditions, seen from the standpoint of their interrelationship, are each different in essence and function and are not intermixed or confused. Therefore, they are said to be different.[1]

The cause, then, in its identity with other causes, is able to create the result totally out of its ability to be a cause, and as such does not differ from any other cause. This same *dharma* also has a different essence because of its particular form and essence; as such, it is not able to create the result without the aid of other exterior conditions working in cooperation with it. "Different essence," in fact, means that it requires the help of these conditions. A simple example will illustrate this. A wheat seed is considered to be the main cause of the new plant, but in order to produce the plant, it needs the aid of sun, water, and soil. The seed has its own essence or nature, while the sun has the nature of heat, the water has the nature of wetness, and the soil has a nutritive and supporting nature. Thus all the elements which participate in the production of the new plant are different in their natures. All must work together, for the seed alone lacks the natures of the other conditions and cannot produce the resulting plant alone. It is different from them.

It is this need for supporting conditions by each causal *dharma* which results in a universally pervasive intercausality which is of the nature of interpenetration of *dharma* and *dharma*. Here it should be noted that although the title of this chapter is "intercausality," this intercausality involves the interpenetration of one thing with another, and Fa-tsang's two major categories of discussion are, in fact, identity and interpenetration. While not ignoring the latter aspect, I have chosen to discuss this part of the system in terms of intercausality in the belief that it would be clearer. By "interpenetration," Fa-tsang means that a *dharma* considered to be the cause includes within it, by a kind of borrowing or usurpation, the qualities possessed by the contributing conditions. In the above analogy of the seed, the seed is said to borrow, and include within itself, the qualities or natures of water, sun, and soil, and only by embracing these qualities in this manner is it able to produce its result. Since any *dharma*, seen from the standpoint of itself, possesses the qualities of all the aiding conditions within itself, and since everything in existence is a condition aiding the one *dharma*, then there is an infinite interpenetration of all *dharmas*.

The analogy of the seed is not completely effective here, because there is unidirectional (or apparently unidirectional) flow of cause from the seed to the result. However, in the more general area of causation, which is the whole universe, the causal flow is multidirectional, and, unlike the seed and the new plant, what is a cause from one standpoint is a result from another, and vice versa. Therefore, the one *dharma* which acts as a cause for the whole is at the same time, as a part of the whole, the result of another cause. What is more, the conditions which aid the cause in producing the result are themselves the result of the causal *dharma*, and these conditions–cum–result are in turn the cause of the causal *dharma*. Interpenetration results from a situation in which the cause includes the conditions within itself while at the same time, being a result itself of other causes, its qualities are being absorbed into the other. Abstractly speaking, the part includes the whole while the whole includes the part. Finally, the whole which is included in the one part is already a whole which includes the part, so that the interpenetration of *dharma* and *dharma* is repeated over and over, infinitely.

It will be recalled that in the analogy of the ten coins, identity of *dharma* with *dharma* was established on the basis of the possession of each *dharma* of the qualities of emptiness and existence. Here, the issue is not identity but the dynamic interaction among these same *dharmas*. Intercausality and interpenetration result from the possession of each *dharma* of the traits of *possessing power* and *not possessing power* to create the result. When we speak of a *dharma* functioning as cause by absorbing the power of the conditions within itself, the cause is then said to possess causal power while the conditions which are absorbed in it are said to be lacking in power. This obviously is simply a way of emphasizing the centrality and importance of the one *dharma* in the nexus of cause and result, because the same *dharma* is also said to be without power, and this means that from another standpoint, this one *dharma* is also the result of another cause or many causes. The new cause has power while the *dharma* previously considered to be a cause is without power, and this is because the cause is now being seen from a new standpoint. In short, a *dharma* both possesses power and lacks power, depending on whether it is being considered as the cause or, from a different angle, part of the result of another cause.

A concrete example of this may be seen in the twelve-linked chain of interdependence, which was used earlier to demonstrate the identity of the twelve links. It is a good example, because traditionally the twelve links have been interpreted as existing simultaneously and interdependently. Now, in terms of power and lack of power, if we start (purely arbitrarily) with *avidyā*, and consider it to be the cause of the entire twelve *dharmas* as a totality, then first it must be said that it is entirely different from the other eleven *dharmas*. A commentary on the Treatise says, "*avidyā* has blindness for its essence, *saṁskāra* has doing for its essence, . . . and old-age and death has termination for its essence."[2] If we now examine the relationship of *avidyā* to the total structure in terms of cause and result, then because *avidyā* is a different sort of thing from the other eleven, in order for it to form the result, it must enlist the aid of these latter *dharmas*. As Fa-tsang says, the qualities of the other *dharmas* are borrowed by the one *dharma*, included in it as its own qualities, and in this way achieves its result. If *avidyā* could create the resultant totality without the aid of these other *dharma*-conditions, the totality itself would be nothing but *avidyā*, in the same way that if my body could be formed solely by my nose, my body would be only a nose. When *avidyā* absorbs these other qualities within itself, it is able to function as *avidyā* and form the result. On the other hand, since *avidyā* itself is created from other *dharmas*, its qualities are also absorbed into them, and interpenetration results from the absorption of all qualities into all twelve *dharmas*. In short, any thing possesses the qualities of all other things. Also, since *avidyā* is part of the result as well as a cause for the result, its usurpation of the power of the other eleven *dharmas* must in part mean that it is able to be *avidyā* and to function as such only because it is given that nature and function through the creative and supportive power of those other *dharmas*.

This picture of a totality which is self-causative, in which each object is always simultaneously exerting power and having its power usurped by other objects, is one in which the usual understanding of such terms as "cause," "condition," and "result" is not at all conventional. There are, in fact, no strict boundaries for these categories, each one being applicable to any object depending on the point of view. Not only does causal power not flow in one direction only, from past to present and present to future, but there is no single locus of causal efficacy. These traditional apprehensions may have some basis, for there is, even in Hua-yen, an acceptance of the fact that the present is a product of the past, and along with a recognition of the temporal nature of one kind of causation, there is a recognition that the seed causes the plant and not vice versa. However, along with more common, "vertical," perceptions of causation there is another, and more important, conception of cause as being a "horizontal" relationship between simultaneously existing things. In this matrix of interdependence, there is no one center of causation; it may be said with equal truth that cause is everywhere and constant, for everything is a cause for everything else.

Fa-tsang's categories of power and lack of power serve no other reason than to rationalize the mutuality of causal power. Looked at from the point of view of a single *dharma* acting as cause for the whole, the conditions (which are also the result) which aid it in forming the result must be considered to be without causal power in order to indicate the ability of this one *dharma* to act as the sole cause for the whole. In other words, the possession of power by the one part shows its absolute necessity in the formation of the whole. A concrete example will make this clearer. In the creation of a totality such as a building, there must be a particular part called a rafter in order for the whole building to exist. Obviously, there must also be other rafters, nails, roof tiles, and so on, all integrated together for there to be a building, but to emphasize the complete necessity of the one rafter for the existence of the building, it is said to possess the causal power to achieve its result. From the standpoint of this rafter, the nails, tiles, and other parts, which act as conditions that aid the rafter, are lacking in power. Their powerlessness, which is their absorption into the causal rafter, highlights the function of the rafter. Only when we turn to the same crucial causal function of a roof tile is the rafter in question now envisioned as without power.

It should not be forgotten in this discussion of the identity and interpenetration of *dharmas* that all these categories—emptiness and existence, power and lack of power, requiring conditions and not requiring conditions, and so on—belong to any entity and to all collectively. It is the one thing, a coin, a rafter, a link in the twelve-linked chain of interdependence, which is all these things at any given instant of time. In fact, there is a startling sameness of qualities and attributes, even in the distinct and different appearances and functions of things. The accompanying diagram will show this clearly. It should be mentioned that the

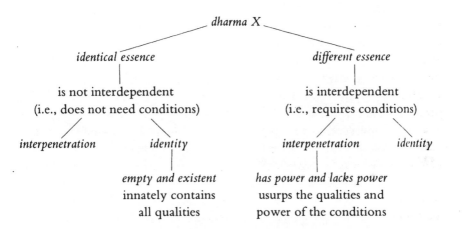

dharma both in its identical essence and different essence is identical with all other *dharmas* and interpenetrates with them, as the diagram shows. The reason for the exact symmetry of qualities is, of course, that whatever the category, the reference is always to one single *dharma*. While the details vary slightly when discussing the category of interpenetration with regard to identical essence, I have dealt with identity in terms of identical essence, and interpenetration with regard to different essence, in accordance with what Fa-tsang and the commentaries themselves say. A noted scholar of Hua-yen, Yusugi Ryōei, says,

> All *dharmas* possess essence and characteristics. Therefore, if you relate *dharma* to *dharma*, as far as essence is concerned, since there are the categories of emptiness and existence, there is the concept of identity. As far as function is concerned, because there are the two categories of possessing power and not possessing power, there is the concept of interpenetration. Taking them together, identical essence and different essence are common to both identity and interpenetration. Taking them separately, identity is related to identical essence, and interpenetration is related to different essence.[3]

The numerous and various qualities and functions of this one *dharma* are intended for no other reason than to attempt to show how things are identical and interpenetrate. Much of any confusion arising from so many categories can be eliminated if it is remembered that Fa-tsang is always talking about the qualities of a *dharma* which enable it to interact with other *dharmas* in such a way as to create the web of interdependency mentioned so often in the preceding chapters.

Therefore, when a *dharma* is said to have an essence both identical with the essences of other *dharmas* and different from those of other *dharmas*, all that is meant is that from the standpoint of causal essence, this one entity is able to produce the cause. For example, the twelve-linked cycle of interdependent being cannot exist without the causal power of karmic preconditions. There is no question of the cooperation of the cause with the other conditions; it is simply a matter of the ability of the one *dharma* to be a cause. However, this is ultimately only half the truth, for the result—the whole cycle—comes into being only when the other eleven *dharmas* assist karmic preconditions. As was mentioned earlier, this is only a recognition of the fact that karmic preconditions have their own unique essence, which is different from that of any of the other eleven elements, and in order for the whole cycle to exist, there must be other elements contributing to the whole. That is to say, karmic preconditions alone cannot produce the whole cycle. Consequently, karmic preconditions have the causal power to produce the result, but this creative function is achieved only when it is aided by the other conditions. However, the fluidity of such terms as "cause," "condition," and "result" becomes clear when it is realized that the so-called result is also the various conditions which aid the cause, and, of course, from another point of view, the result-cum-conditions is the cause for what was previously considered to be the cause. Finally, the full interdependent situation is clarified by the interesting fact that the cause which produces the result is given its causal power by the very result it creates. For instance, in the next chapter, in the analogy of the rafter and the barn of which it is a part, the rafter which creates the barn-result is given its "rafterness"—i.e., its causal power as a distinct and different part—by the barn which it brings into being. This is the real meaning of interdependence.

Finally, to speak of the identity and interdependence of *dharmas* is really only a linguistic convention born of necessity, for "identity" and "interdependence" are simply two expressions for the same phenomenon. The primary, fundamental category of emptiness—if emptiness can be considered a category—is at the base of both these categories. That is, looked at purely from the standpoint of essence, *dharmas* are identical in their emptiness, but from the standpoint of function, this identity in emptiness is itself nothing other than the conditioned, dependent nature of each *dharma*. To use terms from earlier chapters, *dharmas* are said to be identical when examined in their static nature, and to interpenetrate when examined in their dynamic nature.

Essentially, things interact, exerting influences which create and maintain, and in turn are the subject of these same influences. To exist means to function in this manner, and Whitehead's statement to the effect that to exist means to exert causal influence is closely paralleled in the Hua-yen vision of a universe where everything, from an atom to the universe itself, functions as the cause for everything else.[4] In Buddhist terminology, this is the emptiness of things, and if there were anything which is not empty, which is to say anything that is not causal in this manner, then it is really a nonentity. Emptiness does not at all rob existence of its vitality and color, rather, the full, round, solid form of the object and its vigorous life of activity are in reality precisely its emptiness. Its concreteness, discreteness, and true individuality are indeed realities of the most vivid kind, and it is only the *manner* in which this object exists that is an issue, not these qualities.

Such is the picture of things which Fa-tsang has painted for us. Whether it is an accurate picture is not for us to say, because the source of the picture, which is advanced meditation, is not accessible to most of us. It is the product, that is, of a *samādhi*, and not just any *samādhi*, but the *sāgara-mudrā samādhi*, the "*samādhi* which is like the images in the ocean," which was the *samādhi* in which the newly enlightened Buddha beheld the entire universe as one living organism of identical and interdependent parts. It would be well here to reemphasize the teaching of Fa-tsang and his tradition, which is that the Hua-yen philosophy, as the fullest and truest form of the Buddha's own teaching, is completely based on this *samādhi*. It is the special and unique features of this *samādhi* which in fact establishes the Hua-yen tradition as the best of all traditions, according to the Hua-yen masters.

It is said that during the second seven days of the long period during which the newly enlightened Buddha sat beneath the *bodhi* tree, after he had made his famous discovery as to the nature of sentient existence, he entered a *samādhi*. In this *samādhi* he beheld with the "universal eye" the cosmos which has been described here.[5] While he was still in this state of mind, he taught the truth of identity and interdependence. The point is that the truth, the teaching of the Hua-yen tradition, was taught during the actual *samādhi*, and not after emerging from it, as in all other sutras. Consequently, while the partial, incomplete teachings of these other traditions and sutras were the attempt to fit the truth to the feeble faculties of his listeners, and were merely *upāya*, or skillful means, the Hua-yen teachings were uttered in the brilliant clarity of *samādhi*. They are thus complete, full, and direct.

The *samādhi* in question is a very special one to the Hua-yen tradition because of its unique (or presumably unique) ability to reveal the truth of identity and interdependence. Whether in fact only this *samādhi* is able to serve in this capacity is perhaps a matter for debate. Are the various *samādhis* mentioned in various Mahayana sutras different, with different contents, or is there only one *samādhi*, which receives different names in conformity with rhetorical needs? This is not at all clear, nor is even the matter of what Buddhists like Fa-tsang meant by *samādhi*. This is not the place to attempt to settle these questions. According to Fa-tsang, the *sāgara-mudrā samādhi* is special in its ability to reveal the whole truth. We have this truth because the Buddha taught it in its fullness while he was immersed in it.

The nature of the *samādhi*, as well as its ability to reveal a truth normally hidden from us, is indicated by the name, which is figurative and meant to indicate its nature. It is said in the *Avataṁsaka Sūtra* and several other scriptures that when the surface of the great ocean is completely still, unruffled by the wind, all things can be revealed as images on its surface. One text says, "It is just as when the wind blows, waves arise in the great ocean, but when the wind stops, the water becomes clear and still, and there is not a single image which is not revealed on its surface."[6] Another text says that the forms of the Asuras dwelling in the sky are all revealed on its surface. It is a simile for this particular *samādhi* because when the activities of the "normally" functioning mind are stilled, like the waves in the ocean, then all things are revealed to the meditator in brilliant clarity. Since in order to perceive the identity and interdependence of everything demands an extremely radical disruption of the normal categorizing, conceptualizing, symbolizing mechanisms of the human mind, obviously the *sāgara-mudrā samādhi* is understood to be an exceptionally profound state of meditation. I have translated the Sanskrit name (*hai-in san-mei*, in Chinese) as "the *samādhi* which is like the images in the ocean," or "*samādhi* which is like the impressions in the ocean," in conformity with the simile. *Mudrā* is sometimes translated as "seal," which is inaccurate in this context because of the connotations it has in some Indian and Tibetan forms of Buddhism.[7]

Thus the Hua-yen teaching derives, according to Fa-tsang, from the Buddha's *samādhi*. However, the *samādhi* also belongs to the Bodhisattva of advanced status, for his own activities, which are those of a Buddha, must grow out of his own vision, in *sāgara-mudrā samādhi*, of a universe of identical things interpenetrating infinitely. This is why the Hua-yen vision is not available to most of us, who rely for information on sources of knowledge which Buddhism criticizes as erroneous and conducive to anxiety and turmoil. If we wish to share the Hua-yen vision, we need only cultivate the *samādhi* which is like the images of the ocean. That means to become Buddha-like.

6

The Part and the Whole

The last two chapters indicate some of the care and ingenuity with which Fa-tsang established a philosophical foundation for the view of existence which is called Hua-yen. After having done this, he then devotes the final pages of his Treatise to a synthesis of the two aspects of identity and interdependence by means of the analogy of a building and one part of the building.[1] In his analysis of the relationship between the building-whole and a rafter-part, he not only offers us a very complete and informative picture of the view of existence with which he was so occupied throughout his life, but he also answers many of the questions that may have arisen in the course of his discussion of particular aspects of that view when the whole picture may have been lost sight of.

Fa-tsang illustrates the relationship between a part of the whole and the whole itself by means of the analogy of a rafter and the building of which it is a part. Ultimately, we are to understand this analogy as showing the relationship between any part of existence—a blade of grass, a man, an idea—and the totality of existence. However, within the Great Immensity there are many other wholes which also have parts, and so we may understand the same relationships as pertaining between a part of the human body and the whole body, between one nation and all other nations, and so on. It will be evident in this last section that one very important application of Hua-yen principles is in the area of the path or career of the Bodhisattva. Here, where the whole career is conceived as a whole, the question arises as to the relationship between any one phase of that career and the whole career, and in the process of answering this question, some very important concepts in Mahayana Buddhist thought are illuminated. In his concern with questions of practice in the Bodhisattva *mārga*, Fa-tsang was following the precedent of Vasubandhu, who, in his commentary on the first *bhūmi* of the *Daśabhūmika Sūtra*, spoke almost exclusively of identity and interdependence in terms of the stages of the Bodhisattva. However, while concerned primarily with the relationship between phases of the *mārga*, he also added that the same relationships existed among other phenomena as well, "such as the *dharmas, āyatanas,* and *dhātus,* and so on."² In this interesting assertion of the identity and interdependence of the phases of Bodhisattva activity, as well as the general applicability of the idea, we can detect part of the reason for the interest in the *Daśabhūmika Sūtra* and its commentary on the part of the Chinese who constituted the Ti-lun school and for the absorption of the Ti-lun into the later Hua-yen school. The debt of Fa-tsang to the Indian material and to the prior work of the Chinese Ti-lun school is also evident.

The analogy of the building is very brief, and I have translated the entire section, interspersing paragraphs of the translation with my own commentary. These remarks are largely based on Chinese commentaries, but since the same material has been covered in the two previous chapters, and since the Chinese commentaries themselves are very terse and largely silent in this section, my own remarks will be brief.³ The discussion by Fa-tsang is clear and informative and does not really need much commentary. It is, for one who has patiently followed Fa-tsang through the more systematic treatment of earlier sections, extremely rewarding, for in its clear picture of the nature of existence as seen by the Hua-yen masters, it is unrivaled in Hua-yen literature, with the possible exception of the small treatise called "The Golden Lion," also by Fa-tsang.⁴

The Perfect Interpenetration of the Six Characteristics

[507c] The interdependent origination of the six characteristics will be divided [for discussion] into three parts. First, the names [of the six characteristics] will be briefly explained; second, the concepts which have given rise to this doctrine will be shown; third, [this teaching] will be elucidated by means of questions and answers.

First, the names: they are the characteristics of universality, particularity, identity, difference, integration, and disintegration. "Universality" means that the one includes many qualities. "Particularity" means that the many qualities are not identical, because the universal is necessarily made up of many dissimilar particulars. "Identity" means that the many elements [which make up the universal] are not different, because they are identical in forming the one universal. "Difference" means that each element is different from the standpoint of any other element. "Integration" means that [the totality of] interdependent origination is formed as a result of [the collaboration of] these [elements]. "Disintegration" means that each element remains what it is [as an individual with its own characteristics] and is not disturbed [in its own nature].[5]

In his analogy of the building, Fa-tsang will attempt to show that any individual —symbolized here by a rafter—possesses six characteristics, or marks, through the possession of which the relationships of identity and interdependence pertain. Thus any individual, such as the rafter in the building, simultaneously possesses the characteristics of universality, particularity, identity, difference, integration, and disintegration. In other words, then, the rafter will be a particular object with its own clear-cut appearance and function but at the same time will be universal, i.e., *will be the building or totality*, and so on. The "one" which is referred to in the sentence concerning universality is the building or, by extension, any totality.

> Second, the concepts which have given rise to this teaching [of the six characteristics]: this teaching attempts to show such things as the interdependent origination of the *dharma-dhātu*, which is the perfect doctrine of the one vehicle [i.e., Hua-yen], the infinite interpenetration [of all things], the unimpeded identity [of all things], and all other matters including the infinite interrelationship of noumenon and phenomenon, [the interrelationship of phenomenon and phenomenon,] and so on, shown in the symbol of the net of Indra. When these concepts are manifested [in the mind of the Bodhisattva], then when one of the many obstacles [*āvaraṇa*] is overcome, all are overcome, and one acquires the destruction of [moral and intellectual faults, or *kleśa* of] the nine times and ten times. In practicing the virtues, when one is perfected, all are perfected, and with regard to reality, when one [part] is revealed, everything is revealed. All things are endowed with universality and particularity, beginning and end are the same, and when one first arouses the aspiration for enlightenment [*bodhicittotpāda*], one also becomes perfectly enlightened. Indeed, the interdependent origination of the *dharma-dhātu* results from the interfusion of the six characteristics, the simultaneity of cause and result, perfectly free identity, and the fact that the goal is inherent in causal practice. The cause [of enlightenment] is the comprehension and practice, as well as enlightenment, of Samantabhadra, and the result is the infinitude which is revealed in the realm of the ten Buddhas, all the details of which can be found in the *Avataṁsaka Sūtra*.

Some of the implications of this doctrine for practice can be seen in this passage,

and a full discussion will be offered in Chapter 7. What is evident here is that on
the basis of the doctrine of emptiness as it is taught by Hua-yen, when one *kleśa*
is exterminated, all are exterminated, and when one of the Bodhisattva virtues
or perfections is realized, all are realized, and even in the earliest stages of the
Bodhisattva's practice, final perfect enlightenment is, at least in some sense, a
reality. The "nine times and ten times" referred to in this passage are the three
times of past, future, and present as they exist in the past, future, and present,
making nine times, and the ten times are these nine times as they exist in one's
mind in any one moment of time. Samantabhadra is the Bodhisattva who
symbolizes the practices of the Bodhisattva. His vows and practices exemplify
the ideal course of conduct in the aspiring Buddhist in those phases of activity
which are conceived as causes for the ensuing enlightenment-result. This course
of conduct is exemplified by the activities of the youth Sudhana in the final
chapters of the *Avataṁsaka Sūtra*. The result is the knowledge of, and the merging
into, the universe of identity and interdependence, which is the experience of
the perfectly enlightened Buddhas. Samantabhadra occupies a very important
place in the sutra, since that work is primarily concerned with these causal
practices. The vows of Samantabhadra, which must be sincerely duplicated by
each aspirant, who really is Samantabhadra,[6] are as follows:

1. Honor all Buddhas.
2. Praise the *Tathāgatas*.
3. Make offerings to all Buddhas.
4. Confess all past transgressions of the Law.
5. Rejoice in the virtues and happiness of others (*muditā*).
6. Request the Buddha to teach the Dharma.
7. Request the Buddha to dwell in the world.
8. Follow the Dharma.
9. Always to benefit other beings.
10. Turn over one's own accumulated merit to others (*pariṇāmana*).[7]

Third, the elucidation by means of questions and answers. Now, the law of
interdependent origination is common to all situations, but here, briefly,
I shall discuss this through the use of [the analogy of] a building formed by
conditions.

   Question: what is the universal? *Answer*: it is the building. *Question*: that
is nothing but various conditions, such as a rafter; what is the building itself?
Answer: the rafter is the building. Why? Because the rafter by itself totally
makes the building. If you get rid of the rafter, the building is not formed.
When there is a rafter, there is a building.

Question: if the rafter all by itself totally creates the building, then if there are still no roof tiles and other things, how can it [wholly] create the building? [508a] Answer: when there are no tiles and such things, the rafter is not a rafter, so it does not create the building. A nonrafter is a rafter which does not create a building. Now, when I say that the rafter does create it, I am only discussing the ability of a [real] rafter to create it. I am not saying that a nonrafter makes it. Why is that? A rafter is a condition [for the building]. When it has not yet created the building, it is not yet a condition, and therefore it is not a rafter. If it is a [real] rafter, it totally forms [the building]. If it does not totally form it, it is not called a rafter.

This passage makes it abundantly clear that Fa-tsang does in fact assert the identity of the rafter and the building, or, in other words, the part and the whole, or the particular and the universal. Is this nonsense? If there is any social agreement on the use of language at all, then when we speak of a part and a whole, we are speaking of two different things, and the reader may object that the assertion of the identity of the rafter and the building is a lamentable lapse in linguistic precision. However, by this time, the sense in which it can be said that different things are identical should be clear. Moreover, the rafter certainly does not become lost in the building in becoming identical with it. Fa-tsang nowhere denies that in the building there can be seen a piece of wood about eleven feet long which is placed in a diagonal position and which supports terracotta tiles. It cannot be confused with the tiles, metal nails, or a floor board. No, the rafter is clearly observable; it maintains its own appearance and function, and that appearance and function differ from all other appearances and functions. It is there; it is itself; it is nothing other than itself.

However, it is this particular object which Fa-tsang identifies with the building in the clearest of language, and of course in identifying it with the whole, he is identifying it with all other particulars which constitute the building, since, as he argues further on, there is no building apart from these particular pieces. Now, it is a basic position in Buddhism that the individual has no self-existence at all and that any existence it may have is completely dependent on conditions exterior to itself. If we therefore examine the existence of this one object called "rafter," we notice too that it does not exist outside the building of which it is a part and which constitutes the many conditions just referred to. It cannot be argued that the rafter is still a rafter even prior to its inclusion in the potential building, because since the barn symbolizes the totality of existence, it can never be a question of an individual's existence prior to its inclusion into existence. It does not exist, a nonentity, as has been previously mentioned. However, the building is more than an analogy; it is an *example* of the relationships asserted by Hua-yen. Therefore, even though a piece of lumber lying on the ground may eventually become a rafter, it can be said that before its inclusion, it is not a rafter.

What this means, then, is that it is the building into which it is fit which makes it a rafter, in strict accordance with the Buddhist idea of conditioned existence. The building makes it a rafter, but at the same time, it is equally obvious that it is the rafter which acts as a condition for the existence of the building. Also, as Fa-tsang says, the rafter not only acts as a necessary condition for the building, but indeed *becomes* the building or is identical with the building. It is identical in a double sense: first, as Fa-tsang notes, since the building-whole does not exist apart from the condition-particulars such as the rafter, the rafter must be the building, or we must search for a building distinct from such things as rafters, joists, and nails. Second, since each particular which helps to make the building functions identically in a strictly interdependent manner to create the whole, and since, as was noted in regard to the rafter, no part has a real independent existence, each part is identical with any other part in its capacity of being a condition.

But Fa-tsang says that the rafter is not just *a* condition or just *a* cause for the building, it is the *sole* cause. When the rafter becomes a rafter through its integration into the building, the combined powers of the total number of conditions which are called "building" are taken on by the rafter, which then has the total power to create the building. This is what Fa-tsang means when he says that a nonrafter—i.e., a rafter which has not become integrated into the building—cannot be the cause of a building. It is only when all things with the exception of the rafter are there that the rafter truly is a rafter. When all other present conditions cause the rafter to be a rafter, it then has the total power to form the building. If it does not, then there is no entity called "building," at least not a perfect building. Of course, any part of the building we may wish to examine simultaneously acts in the same way. Some of the other questions which may be raised in this passage above will be answered as Fa-tsang continues.

> *Question*: if all the various conditions such as the rafter each exerts [its own] partial power, thus creating [the building] together [through the collaboration of many individual partial powers] and not through total power, what would be the error? *Answer*: there would be the errors of eternalism and annihilationism. If [each part] does not wholly cause [the building] to be made and only exerts partial power, then each condition would have only partial power. They would consist simply of many individual partial powers and would not make one whole building. This is annihilationism [because there could be no building]. Also, the various conditions cannot completely

make the building if they each possess partial power, so that if you maintain that there is [still] a whole building, then since it exists without a cause, this is eternalism. Also, if [the rafter] does not wholly create [the building], then when the one rafter is removed, the whole building should remain. However, since the total building is not formed, then you should understand that the building is not formed by the partial power [of a condition such as the rafter] but by its total power.

In this defense of his earlier statements, Fa-tsang resorts to a traditional Buddhist method of argument which consists of showing that if a certain position is carried to its logical conclusion, the result will be the positions of eternalism and annihilationism, the two extremes. The former is the position which holds that an entity exists in its own right independent of conditions, while the latter position involves a view of destruction, negation, and annihilation. The correct position as far as Buddhism is concerned is the well-known "Middle Way," which makes neither an unqualified affirmation nor an unqualified negation vis-à-vis a given situation. Thus, as has been argued throughout the Treatise, existence is neither negated or denied, nor is it naively affirmed as existing absolutely in its own right. Rather, when certain conditions are prevalent, a result will come into being, and that entity will continue to exist and to evolve in a certain manner as long as the necessary conditions are there. Existence therefore is neither absolutely existent, nor is it nonexistent; it is contingently existent, and it is because of contingent or dependent being that progress in the Dharma is possible.

Here, for the most part, Fa-tsang is concerned with arguing that the particular individual possesses total power to create the whole. The argument seems to be simple enough; if the rafter does not have this total power, then if the rafter is removed, the whole building should remain, just as my whole body should remain if a leg is amputated. Obviously this is not the case, and so Fa-tsang says that in order for the whole to be a whole, the part must exert total power in the formation of the whole. To possess total power means, as was said above, the causative power of the whole building. Partial power, on the other hand, is simply the power in the rafter itself. What this really means, presumably, is that if the rafter were to exert only the causative power of itself—i.e., to exert the power of its rafterness—then it could never truly become integrated into the total building and become the building. In this case, no building would be possible. However, once integrated into the whole building, the rafter assumes the causative power of the whole building and thus acts as total cause for it. This is, in fact, nothing more than the kind of true interdependence which Hua-yen teaches.

Question: why would there be no building if a single rafter is lacking? *Answer*: that would only be a spoiled building, not a perfect building. Therefore, you should know that the perfect building is inherent in the one rafter. Since it is inherent in this one rafter, you should know therefore that the rafter is the building. *Question*: since the building is identical with the rafter, then the remaining planks, tiles, and so on, must be identical with the rafter, aren't they? *Answer*: generally speaking, they are all identical with the rafter. The reason is that if you take away a rafter, there is no building, because if there is no rafter, the building is spoiled. And when you have a spoiled building, you cannot speak of planks, tiles, and so on. Therefore, the planks, tiles, and so on, are identical with the rafter. If they are not the rafter, then the building is not formed, for planks, tiles, and so on, do not become formed either. Now, since they all are formed together, you should know that they are identical [with the rafter]. Since this is so of the one rafter, the other rafters are the same. Therefore, if all the *dharmas* which constitute interdependent origination are not formed [as an integrated totality of interdependence], then they cease. If they are all formed [together], then they are all identical with each other, interfused, completely free in their interrelationships, extremely difficult to conceive, and surpass commonsense notions. The nature of things, which is interdependent origination, is universal, so you can understand everything else by analogy with the above example.

In this passage, which speaks of taking a rafter away from the building, there is some possibility of misreading Fa-tsang's intention. As has been mentioned several times, there is really no question of removing the part from the whole, at least if the whole is the whole of existence. Whether the whole be the greatest of wholes, or the body of a mouse, when a part is removed, the previously perfect whole is destroyed; it just is not *that* particular whole any more. The perfect whole is implied in the part in the sense that the whole becomes the whole only when the part is integrated into it and becomes the whole. If a part is removed, the previous whole now becomes a new whole and still the question of the relationship of the existent parts remains, because Hua-yen is concerned only with the question of the relationship pertaining among entities. Actually, even the disappearance of an entity acts as a condition for the whole and thus changes the configuration of the whole in some way, as was noted by John Donne, who said that "any man's death diminishes me, because I am involved in mankind." Death, disappearance, diminution—all these are events also, and constitute those conditions by which I *am* and by which I am defined. Moreover, the new appearance of an entity acts as a condition in the same way, not only affecting the present and future, but even the past, in the same way, according to T.S. Eliot, that a new poem retrospectively changes the whole history of literature as far back as the creation of the first poem.

The last part of the preceding paragraph from the Treatise may be obscure partly because it is so terse and elliptical. However, if we keep in mind that the identity of the parts is due to their emptiness, and this emptiness is none other than the interdependence of these parts, much of the difficulty will be removed. The argument, paraphrased, is this: if the rafter is not integrated into the whole building, then we cannot speak of tiles, nails, and the like, since they derive their existence from the existence of the rafter. The assemblage of particulars which is called "building" and the one particular called "rafter" thus act as necessary conditions for the existence of the other; they have no independent existence at all in this interdependence, and it is this universal lack of self-existence which constitutes their identity. Thus, as Fa-tsang says, "if all the *dharmas* which constitute interdependent origination are not formed [as an integrated totality of interdependence], then they cease." To use another analogy, my "fatherness" is completely dependence on the "sonness" of my son to the same extent that his "sonness" is dependent on my "fatherness." He is not a son without the father, and the father is not a father without him. In this way, the two existences arise together in strict interdependence, or neither existence is possible.

> Second, the characteristic of particularity: all the conditions such as the rafter are parts in the whole. If they were not parts, they could not form a whole, because without parts, there is no whole. What this means is that intrinsically the whole is formed of parts, so that without parts, there can be no whole. Therefore, the parts become parts by means of the whole. *Question*: if the whole is identical with the parts, how can it be a whole? *Answer*: it can be a whole precisely because it is identical with the parts. Just as the rafter is identical with the building, which is called the characteristic of universality [possessed by the rafter-part], so also because it is a rafter, we speak of the characteristic of particularity. If the rafter is not identical with the building, it is not a rafter; if [the building] is not identical with the rafter, it is not a building. The universal and the particular are identical. [508b] This is how you should understand it.
>
> *Question*: if they are identical, how can you [even] speak of parts? *Answer*: because [parts] become parts on the basis of their identity [with the whole]. If they [i.e., part and whole] were not identical, the whole would exist outside the parts, and could not then be a whole; the parts would exist

outside the whole and could not then be parts. If you think about it, it is clear.

Question: what would the error be if they are not parts? *Answer*: the errors of annihilationism and eternalism. If there were no parts, there would be no distinct rafters, tiles, and so on. This would be annihilationism, because without distinct parts such as rafters, tiles, and so on, there would be no building. If it is maintained that there can still be a building without distinct rafters, tiles, and the like, this is eternalism.

With the discussion of the characteristic of particularity, the major portion of Fa-tsang's demonstration is complete, and the following sections dealing with the other four characteristics serve primarily to illuminate certain details. The last two pairs of characteristics—identity and difference, and integration and disintegration—repeat the first pair inasmuch as they are concerned with the relationship of the part and the whole. The commentaries discuss each of the three pairs of characteristics with one of the so-called "three greats," or three major aspects of the absolute.

universality—particularity = essence
identity—difference   = characteristics
integration—disintegration = function

While each of the three pairs of characteristics shows a different way of viewing existence, it is clear from the commentaries that in the above list all the items in the first row—universality, identity, and integration—stress the essential one-ness and interpenetration of the many, while the items in the second row—particularity, difference, and disintegration—stress the many.[8] Thus, while Fa-tsang moves on to a new pair of seemingly contrary characteristics, he is still showing the simultaneous oneness and manyness of existence.

The question which is raised in this passage is how one can speak of parts when it has been said that the part is the whole. Fa-tsang's answer is the soul of simplicity: a whole is necessarily composed of parts, and to speak of parts is to imply that they are parts of a whole. The one does not exist apart from the other. If they do, then the whole has an existence independent of parts, which is the error of eternalism, and the part is not part of anything, which is nonsense. Again, the interdependence existing between the part and the whole is pointed out in the statement that "the parts become parts by means of the whole," which simply means that when the part becomes integrated into the whole, and con-sequently becomes the whole, it is sustained by the whole in its very act of creating the whole.

Third, the characteristic of identity: the various conditions such as the rafter all combine and create the building. Because there is no difference among them [as conditions], all are called "conditions of the building." This is called the characteristic of identity because they are all identically conditions within the context of the building which they create. *Question*: what is the difference between this and the [above] characteristic of universality? *Answer*: the characteristic of universality is spoken of only from the standpoint of the one [whole] building; the characteristic of identity concerns all the various conditions such as the rafter. Even though each part is different in its own nature, they each possess the characteristic of identity because they are all identical in their power of creation. *Question*: what is the error if they are not identical? *Answer*: the errors of annihilationism and eternalism. If they are not identical, the [particular] conditions such as the rafter would oppose each other, and thus would not be able to create the building identically. This is annihilationism, because there would be no building. If [on the other hand] they cannot create the building, because each is different, and you still say that there is a building, this is eternalism, because there is a building without any cause.

The difference between the characteristics of universality and identity is that universality refers to the relationship between the part and the whole *qua* whole and to the situation by which the part is universalized by its inclusion in the whole. Identity, on the other hand, stresses the relationship between a part and any other part. In particular, identity stresses the fact that any part is interchangeable with another part by virtue of their both being conditions for the whole. The emperor of China and a sand flea are thus identical in the sense that they are both empty, both interdependent, both conditions for the totality of existence. Is there no difference at all? The differences which we detect and emphasize are subjective interpretations, our own self-interested values imposed on what is otherwise a valuative no-man's land.

Fourth, the characteristic of difference: the various conditions such as the rafter are different from each other in conformity with their own individual species. *Question*: if they are different, how can they be identical? *Answer*: they are identical precisely because they are different. If they were not different, then since the rafter is [about] eleven feet long, the tiles would be the same, and since this would destroy the original condition [i.e., the tile as it should be], then, as before, they could not function identically as conditions for the building. Now, since there is a building, they must all function identically as conditions, and so you can understand that they are different.

Question: what is the difference between this and the characteristic of particularity? *Answer*: particularity means that all the conditions, such as the rafter, are distinct within the one building. Now, when we speak of difference, we mean that each of the various conditions, such as the rafter, are different from each other.

Question: what is the error if they are not difference [from each other]? *Answer*: there would be the errors of annihilationism and eternalism. If they are not different, then [as I have said,] the roof tiles would be [about] eleven feet long, like the rafter. This would destroy the original condition [of the tile] and the building could not be formed. Therefore, you have annihilationism. Eternalism results from attachment to the existence of a building which has no conditions, because if the various conditions are not different, then the necessary conditions for the building do not exist.

This passage should dispel any mistaken understanding of the idea of identity as removing the differences between things, because here Fa-tsang says quite clearly that things are identical just because they are different. Implicit here is the feeling on the part of Buddhists such as Fa-tsang that everything in its almost bewildering variety is good just as it is (or perhaps, we should say, Good), for the existence we know would not be possible without this variety.

Fifth, the characteristic of integration: because the building is created as a result of these various conditions, the rafter and other parts are called conditions. If this were not so, neither of the two [i.e., forming conditions or formed result] would come to be. Now, since they actually form [the building], you should know that this is the characteristic of integration.

Question: [508c] when we actually see the various conditions such as the rafter, each retains its own character and does not literally become a building; how is it able to form the building? *Answer*: simply because the various conditions such as the rafter do not become [the building, and retain their own character], they are able to create the building. The reason for this is that if the rafter becomes the building, it loses its intrinsic character of being a rafter, and therefore the building cannot come into being. Now, because it does not become [the building], conditions such as the rafter and so on are manifested. Because they are manifested [as being just what they are], the building is created. Also, if they do not make the building, the rafters and so on are not to be called conditions. However, since they can be said to be conditions, you should know that they definitely create the house.

Question: if they do not become integrated, what is the error? *Answer*: the errors of annihilationism and eternalism. Why? The building is created originally as a result of the various conditions such as the rafter. Now, if they do not create the building all together [in their integration], the existence of the building is not possible, and this is annihilationism. Originally, the conditions create the building, and thus they are called rafters and so on. Now, since [hypothetically] they do not create the building, they are not rafters, and this [also] is annihilationism. If they do not become integrated, then because a building exists without a cause, this is eternalism. It is also eternalism if the rafters do not create the building but are still called rafters.

Sixth, the characteristic of disintegration: each of the various conditions such as the rafter retains its own separate character [i.e., *svadharma*] and does not [literally] become [the building]. *Question*: if you see the various conditions such as the rafter right in front of you, creating and perfecting the building [i.e., integrated into the building], how can you say that they do not intrinsically become [the building]? *Answer*: simply because they do not become [the building], the *dharma* or building can be formed. If they [actually] become the building and do not retain their own characters, then the building cannot come into being. Why? Because if they [literally] become [the building], they lose their [individual] characters, and the building cannot be formed. Now, since the building is formed, you should know that they do not [literally] become [the building].

Question: if they were to become the building, what would be the error? *Answer*: there would be the errors of annihilationism and eternalism. If it is claimed that the rafter [literally] becomes the building, the character of rafterness is lost. Because the character of the rafter is lost, the building has no conditions [for its existence] and cannot exist. This is annihilationism. If the character of the rafter is lost, and yet a building were able to exist, this would be eternalism, because the building would exist without conditions.

Also, universality is the one building, particularity consists of the various conditions, identity is the nondifference [of the parts as conditions for the whole], difference is the difference of the various conditions [from the standpoint of each other], integration means that the various conditions create the result, and disintegration means that each [condition] retains its own character. To summarize this in a verse:

The many in the one is the characteristic of universality;

The many not being the one is the characteristic of particularity;

[509a] The universal is formed by many species which are in themselves identical;

Their identity is shown in the difference of each in its own essence;

The principle of the interdependent origination of the one and the many is wonderful integration;

Disintegration means that each retains its own character and does not become [the whole].

This all belongs to the realm of [Buddha-] wisdom and is not said from the standpoint of worldly knowledge.

By means of this skillful device [of the teaching of the six characteristics], you can understand Hua-yen.

With this verse, the Treatise comes to an end with the hope on Fa-tsang's part that this teaching of the six characteristics will help us understand the Hua-yen view of things. Let us hope this wish has not been in vain, for the teaching of the six characteristics is one of the important rubrics of the Hua-yen system, and if Fa-tsang has failed to clarify his vision by means of this teaching, then we also will have failed to understand the system itself. The vision that Fa-tsang shows us here is not difficult to understand if we bear in mind that it is nothing but the Chinese Buddhist way of handling the classic Buddhist doctrine of interdependent origination, which is another way of saying "Emptiness." Nothing which has been said in the above passages will seem strange or fantastic to anyone who has a firm grasp on the emptiness doctrine. Such a vision as has been presented to us is not even to be thought of as mystic, in the strict sense of the word. If the mystic effort lifts the individual above the world of cause and effect to a vision of things unearthly and beyond change, with a corollary rejection of the world as completely deficient, then Hua-yen is not at all mystical in its apprehension of the world of identity and interdependence. It is true, as has been remarked several times, that this vision is apprehended only by those who have transcended *themselves*, but such a self-transcendence does not involve a transcendence of the world itself. On the contrary, the effort of self-transcendence, by which egotism, pride, and delusion are destroyed, is accompanied by a parallel immersion even more deeply than before into the concrete world of things. Rather than banish things as unworthy, such a vision reinstates the common and ordinary (as well as the "horrible" and "disgusting") to a position of ultimate value. The Hua-yen vision thus entails both a loss and a gain. The loss is the loss of the intruding self, which will not let things be what they are.

The gain is the new ability to see that everything is wonderful and good (or Good). The world is a Good place, even with its tigers, disease, and death. The loss and gain are one and the same thing, just as when one side of the scale sinks down, the other side comes up. In this event, the Buddhist can say of any day, whether it is the day he was born, the day he became enlightened, or the day he dies, that "every day is a Good day."

7

Vairocana

Towering over the broad, flat plain of Nara, a few miles south of Kyoto, Tōdai-ji still maintains much of the grandeur and dignity of a temple which was conceived as the national cathedral of Japan back in the days when Nara was the capital. The visitor at Tōdai-ji approaches it on a long stone walk which is lined with trees and open parks. Walking leisurely along the path through a succession of · huge gates, the visitor has the impression of being part of one of those stately processions to the temple that passed through these gates in the days of Nara's glory. Passing through the Middle Gate, the visitor stands somewhat awed before the Hall of the Great Buddha. Over 159 feet high and 187 feet wide, it is the largest standing wooden building in the world. When he now crosses the last open courtyard and passes from the bright Japanese sun into the cool, dim interior, he is confronted with an even more impressive sight. It is the massive bronze figure of the sitting Buddha, Vairocana, 53.1 feet high. He sits on an open lotus in true Buddha fashion, with legs crossed in the traditional manner, his right hand extended palm out in the gesture of removing fear, his left hand lying palm up in his lap. His half-closed eyes indicate that he is in profound *samādhi*, and the faint smile on his lips, indicating his unfathomable bliss, taunts the foolish worldling caught up in the treadmill of life. The whole figure is circled with an aureole, much like the halo around the head of a Christian saint, and imbedded in the aureole, as if radiating from the central figure, there can be seen many other smaller Buddhas, sitting in identical fashion.

The traveler who has seen many of the impressive sights of Japan is nevertheless still very impressed by the overwhelming figure of Vairocana, and rightly so, because the figure was meant to impress. Tōdai-ji is the central temple of the Japanese branch of Hua-yen Buddhism, and Vairocana is the cosmic Buddha, whose body is infinitely large, and whose life is infinitely long. In fact, the Hua-yen universe which has been described in the foregoing pages is said to be the very body of this Buddha, and his presence shines sublimely forth from every particle in the universe. Hence his name, Vairocana, the Buddha of Great Illumination, whose light shines into every corner of the universe. A pamphlet which the visitor receives at Tōdai-ji informs him that "Vairocana Buddha exists everywhere and every time in the universe, and the universe itself is his body. At the same time, the songs of birds, the colors of flowers, the currents of streams, the figures of clouds—all these are the sermon of Buddha."[1] He thus preaches his wisdom constantly and eternally for the salvation of all beings. Tu-shun, the first patriarch of Chinese Hua-yen says,

> The past practices of the Buddha Vairocana
> Cause oceans of Buddha-lands to be purified.
> Immeasurable, incalculable, infinite,
> He freely pervades all places.
> The Dharma-body of the *Tathāgata* is inconceivable;
> It is formless, markless, and incomparable.
> He manifests a form and marks for the sake of living beings
> And there is no place he is not manifested.
> In all the atoms of all Buddha-lands,
> Vairocana displays his sovereign might.
> He vows with the earth-shaking sounds of oceans of Buddhas
> To tame every kind of living being.[2]

This universal and eternal pervasiveness is symbolized by the many images in the aureole surrounding, and emanating from, the Great Buddha of Nara. Each smaller Buddha is one of the infinity of things which constitute the universe, and is nothing but the reality of Vairocana himself, shining forth as each entity.

The *dharma-dhātu* of identity and interdependence which was described in previous chapters is thus none other than the body of Vairocana. How are we to understand this? Has the intricate and careful philosophy of Hua-yen become sullied with some absurd species of pantheism? Did rational men such as Fa-tsang really believe that the universe was in the form of a gigantic being, similar to the cosmic *puruṣa* of the ancient Indian non-Buddhist literature? Certainly the language of the Hua-yen spokesmen exemplified in the above passages, as well as many more, support such a supposition. In some sense, at least, Vairocana, a Buddha, is coterminous with the material universe.

Of course the problem of pantheism, strictly defined, is no issue here at all. Whatever Vairocana is, he is not a god, nor has he any of the functions of a god such as conceived by the main Western monotheistic religions (or even Indian religions). He is not the creator of the universe, he does not judge either the living or the dead, nor is he a stern but just father who governs the activities of his children. One cannot bargain with Vairocana or petition him for special favors, since nothing can transgress the law that says that what is going to be is going to be. Vairocana, like the Tao, is ruthless; it is pointless to pray to him, love him, fear him, or flee him, for Vairocana is not that sort of being. In short, Vairocana is not a god, so there is no question of Hua-yen holding some notion that everything is god. He is not even a "he."

Sometimes, however, and with a little more justification, some scholars of both the East and the West have referred to Hua-yen and similar types of Buddhism as "pan-Buddhism"; i.e., they hold that everything is the Buddha, or that the Buddha is everywhere. This resembles the language of the above passages. Certainly Vairocana is a Buddha, and it is said that he exists in all places at all times. In his Treatise, Fa-tsang speaks of Vairocana as the "Buddha with the ten bodies," and since Hua-yen habitually uses the number ten to symbolize infinity, this is another way of saying that Vairocana is omnipresent.[3] Thus flatly stated without qualification, Hua-yen is certainly a type of pan-Buddhism. The infinite universe is his body, and every particle of the universe, however minute or humble, constantly teaches the Dharma with his voice. The Sung dynasty poet Su Tung-p'o says,

> The sounds of valley streams are his long, broad tongue;
> The forms of the mountains are his pure body.
> At night, I hear the myriad hymns of praise;
> How can I tell men what they say?[4]

The question is not whether Vairocana *is* the universe, or perhaps is *in* the universe. That he is the universe is clearly shown by all the literature, and the Great Buddha of Nara shows it most graphically in monumental bronze. The real question is, *in what sense* is Vairocana the universe? This is a good opportunity to look into the question not only of who or what Vairocana is, but also what a "Buddha" meant to Buddhists of the Sino-Japanese tradition.

It is very easy to interpret such passages as the above advocating some kind of animism or a view of nature as possessing some kind of metaphysical substance. The problem derives partly from the language of Hua-yen literature and partly from the common Western categories by which we think. Western people, reared in a tradition which conceives of the holy as always the totally other, a separate, transcendent deity who abides apart from his own creation, tend to interpret systems of thought such as the Hua-yen as holding a view of two distinct orders of being, in which there is some divine being which acts as the true substance or essence underlying an outward, phenomenal level of reality. The picture we get is, to state it crudely, of hollow objects inhabited by some kind of spirit. The spirit is a "ghost in the machine" which gives life and meaning to otherwise senseless, lifeless machines. Therefore, when told that the universe is the body of Vairocana, we naturally construe this as meaning that Vairocana is one sort of thing and that the universe is another, and that Vairocana is a divine being who dwells in men, trees, animals, rocks, and so forth. But this is not the way in which we should understand Vairocana.

The language of Hua-yen texts seems to support an animistic or "pantheistic" interpretation, without doubt, and part of the purpose of this chapter is to investigate this language and its meaning. For instance, a metaphor which Hua-yen uses, derived from the common stock of Mahayana Buddhist figures of speech, is that of the water and the wave, used to illustrate the relationship between the absolute and the phenomenal. Under the influence of wind, the water becomes disturbed and forms waves. Here, water stands for the absolute, and waves stand for the phenomenal manifestation in time and space of this absolute. Thus, while we see waves, their true substance is the water. However, even though water manifests itself as waves, it never loses its intrinsic nature as water. At the same time, it indubitably appears as waves. In fact, says Fa-tsang, if it did not retain its water nature, it could not become waves. This is very similar to the language of the *Awakening of Faith in the Mahāyāna*, which says that "as a result of the winds of ignorance, Mind which is intrinsically pure becomes agitated and forms waves."⁵ In the use of the metaphor, as well as its use in the *Awakening of Faith* and other texts, the meaning seems to be that there is some metaphysical substance, more real, true, and pure, which underlies the outward appearance of things.

Another image is that of gold and the forms taken by this gold. Fa-tsang says,

> Gold has the two aspects of immutability and conditionedness. It has the meaning of immutability because it does not lose its weight [i.e., does not become diminished in its uses]. It has the meaning of conditionedness because it easily becomes finger rings [and the like]. Also, the ring has the two meanings of emptiness and manifestation. It has no existence apart from the gold, so it is empty. It is manifested because the ring looks like a ring. Now, because the emptiness of the ring is dependent on the immutability of the gold, even though the ring may lose its form as a ring, the gold is not diminished. Consequently, living beings are the Dharmabody [of Vairocana]. Also, because the manifestation of the ring is dependent

on the gold's obedience to conditions, the whole essence of the gold is manifested as a ring. Therefore, the Dharma-body [of Vairocana] becomes living beings [and other things].[6]

Here, as in the analogy of the water and the waves, the meaning seems to be that Vairocana is the substance underlying phenomenal reality. Living beings (and nonliving beings) are the Dharma-body of the Buddha. In these two metaphors, another element is also added which complicates understanding. Both metaphors speak of a reality which presumably is antecedent to the world of things which it becomes. First there is water, then it manifests itself as waves; first there is gold, then it becomes necklaces, rings, and so on. There is thus, along with the tendency to conceive of Vairocana as a substance, a corollary tendency to see Hua-yen as teaching a kind of emanationism, in which the universe is considered to be the efflux or emanation of a pure, solitary, unmoved prior Being. This is a serious error also, for then we imagine that there was some primordial deity, similar to Brahman of the *Upaniṣads*, who, for some inscrutable reason, manifested himself as the present phenomenal universe which we see about us and of which we are a part.

This same impression can be had from much of Fa-tsang's systematic presentation of his philosophy, and it will be recalled that in Chapter 4, where Fa-tsang's ideas on identity were discussed, the very basis of Hua-yen thought seems to be a view of an Absolute which existed prior in time to a concrete world of things (*shih*) which it *became*. There it was said that any phenomenal object is a mixture of the True and the false, or the Unconditioned and conditioned. (Of course, the sum total of all things is this same mixture.) Taking up the absolute side of things first, Fa-tsang says that it itself has two aspects. First, he says, it is immutable. This is not surprising, because all religions claim immutability as the nature of the absolute. What kind of absolute would it be which changed just like the ordinary things of the world? Being immutable, the absolute is forever unmoved, pure, eternal, still, and serene. This is, in fact, a common description of the absolute in all Mahayana forms of Buddhism. However, Fa-tsang next says something which not only seems to contradict this statement, but which also is very unusual in Buddhism; he says that moved by certain conditions, this pure, unmoved, eternal Reality changes and appears as the universe of phenomenal objects.[7] However, like the gold which has become a ring, the immutable absolute remains the immutable absolute. Here again the picture is apparently one of the emanation of the concrete universe from an immutable absolute, with the result that things are a mixture of the absolute and phenomenal.

The analogy of the gold and the ring mentioned another aspect of reality also, its concrete existence as "things." In his Treatise, Fa-tsang turns from his analysis of the absolute to phenomenal things themselves, and here too he finds a dual aspect. When we gaze at the world around us, we in fact see no absolute at all. This is the everyday experience of most of us, in which we perceive a world of ordinary things, probably totally lacking in anything we would construe as being noumenous. Rocks, trees, mountains, stars, men, and animals—these, we realize, come into existence, survive a while, and then disappear forever. They do, however, seem to be solid enough to the perceiver, who is reluctant to deny their existence "out there" beyond his own mind and body. He gives the real-looking rock a kick, as did Samuel Johnson when he kicked the rock in order to refute Berkeleian idealism for his friend Boswell, and exclaims, "It feels real enough to me!" The Buddhist foot encounters something just as Johnson's foot did. It is there, just as the ring is there in the analogy, and there is no gainsaying the sudden pain in one's toes. Fa-tsang calls this quality of things "quasi-existence," by which he means that entities *seem* to be as existent as the absolute is. In other words, this is the commonsense solidness and reality of ordinary experience, and it is really "there."

Along with this concreteness there is another aspect of phenomena which Fa-tsang calls emptiness, the emptiness which was discussed in an earlier chapter devoted to indigenous Indian Buddhist concepts. That is, things do not exist in their own right, independently, but rather exist only in dependence upon something else. When the Buddhist subjects the solid rock to a careful scrutiny, he finds nothing about the rock which would give it an independent existence. It is lacking in a *svabhāva*, an independence or self-existence which would allow it to exist apart from any contributing or supporting conditions. This is its emptiness; it is nothing but its *complete* dependence on conditions for its own existence. Needless to say, it also serves as a condition for others. At any rate, we can see that an entity, or concrete fact of experience, has a dual nature in the same way that the absolute does. A simple chart will show the two aspects of both the absolute and the phenomenal (what Chinese frequently refer to as *li* and *shih* respectively).

Absolute $\begin{cases} \text{Immutability} \\ \text{Conditionedness} \end{cases}$

Phenomenal $\begin{cases} \text{Quasi-existence} \\ \text{Emptiness} \end{cases}$

If we keep in mind one of the major Hua-yen premises, that the immutable absolute becomes conditioned and appears as phenomenal existence, it will be clear that there is a close relationship between the two aspects of the absolute and the two of the phenomenal world. In fact, what Fa-tsang calls "quasi-existence," the seeming ultimacy of concrete facts, is none other than the conditionedness of the absolute, and the empty nature of this same concrete reality is really nothing other than the immutability ascribed to the absolute. In reality, what seems to be several aspects of two levels of reality is only one single reality, and what is seen as the ordinary, everyday world of things is indeed that, but at the same time, its true nature is its immutable, absolute nature. Again, we have a view of existence which sees things as being an intersection of the True and the false, the Absolute and relative, the Unconditioned and the conditioned. Fa-tsang says the same thing many times in his writings. In his long commentary on the *Avataṁsaka Sūtra*, the *T'an hsüan chi*, he says that the absolute, in obedience to conditions, becomes different things, and these different things are not apart from the absolute.[8] Other examples are abundant.

Does this sort of language really mean what it seems to? If Hua-yen Buddhism indeed holds to a view of the emanation of the phenomenal world from a prior existing absolute, as well as a view of things as consequently possessing this metaphysical substance, then Hua-yen Buddhism has strayed far away from its Indian parent. However, I doubt whether any form of Chinese or Japanese Buddhism has ever, at least outside the popular understanding, held such views, language notwithstanding. In all the varieties of forms which Buddhism has assumed in its 2,500-year history, one of the common elements which has bound these diverse forms together has been the consistent and insistent denial of any kind of essence in things, including a divine or transcendental essence. The doctrine of the emptiness of all things is the very cornerstone of Buddhist philosophy and practice, and despite the occurrence of "Seed of Buddhahood" (*tathāgatagarbha*), "Store Consciousness" (*ālaya-vijñāna*), and other doctrines similar to these, Buddhists have always insisted (rightly I believe) that these should not be mistaken for metaphysical substances, spirits, and the like. We would probably better understand Buddhism if we took their protestations seriously. Much of the problem of understanding begins with our failure to grasp the very fundamentals of Buddhism.

Part of the problem with understanding Hua-yen lies in its habitual use of such terms as "immutable," "existence," and "nonexistence." Although we may take it for granted that the words must mean what they seem to mean, the truth of the matter is that Buddhists often use such terms in different ways than do Westerners. A case in point is "nonexistence" (Chin. *wu*). Now, nonexistence stands in opposition to existence, and if I can be said to exist now, my nonexistence would seem to be the complete negation of this state of beingness. Nonbeing is thus similar to the mathematical zero, and denotes voidness, vacuity, or the barrenness of any given locus. We usually associate nonexistence with privation of some sort, and the corresponding attitude is one of fear, dislike, and disgust. My own potential nonexistence thus fills me with fear and loathing, the non-existence of money in my pocket arouses emotions of dislike, anxiety, and the like. Or there may be the nonexistence of pain, poverty, and death, in which case the corresponding emotion may be one of gratitude or gladness. At any rate, nonexistence denotes the complete absence of something from some place. It means that there is a kind of hole in existence some place (maybe in all places), and there is no positive value in this hole. However, the Sino-Japanese Buddhist tradition uses the term "nonexistence" to stand for a state of optimum fullness. It is a state of overbrimming potential for creativity, and it is, in fact, another word for the absolute.[9] Without this nonexistence there could not for a second be any existence, and so rather than denoting denial or privation, it denotes something positive. It is what might be called "warm" in its connotations, and the Buddhist's emotional response to the word is often the same as the Westerner's response to the word "God." Thus awareness of the nonexistence which is thoroughly mixed with existence is not a cause for some Kierkegaardian anxiety; it is cause rather for gratitude, confidence, and perhaps even love, in the con-templation of the very root source of everything which exists. It will be recalled that Taoists such as Lao-tzu and Chuang-tzu usually referred to the absolute as "nonexistence" in the knowledge that this absolute was *not an existent*, or *not a thing*, in the same way that a man, a thought, or an abstraction such as time is a *thing*. If it is not a thing, what better name for it than "no thing"?

Thus "nonexistence" means something other than what we would think it meant. The same applies to other common Hua-yen terms, such as "immutable." The word means, for most people, "nonchanging," and we tend to think therefore of a static entity of some kind, for how can something be both unchang-ing and dynamic at the same time? When Fa-tsang says that the immutable absolute transforms itself into phenomenal objects but at the same time retains its immutability, we tend to conclude that the absolute must be a static entity which lurks beneath the surface of its changing surface appearances. The mental picture is somewhat like the popular Western concert of the soul; though the body-shell grows old, suffers sickness and injury, and finally dies, the inner soul, the real "me," is eternal and immutable. The only apparent difference is that whereas the Western soul is always individual and distinct, the Buddhist equiv-alent is one single essence common to all entities. This interpretation is reinforced in Hua-yen writings by the tendency to equate the immutable absolute *qua* absolute with existence, and to equate phenomenal reality *qua* absolute with nonexistence or emptiness. Therefore, when we are told that phenomenal reality is empty, we make the logical jump of concluding that the real reality of entities must be an immutable substance or spirit of some sort. This is entirely possible due to such passages as the following:

> *Tathatā* [i.e., the absolute, Vairocana] has the meaning of existence, because it is the basis of error and enlightenment. Also it means nonempty, because it is indestructible.... Also, *tathatā* means emptiness, because it is divorced from characteristics, because it obeys conditions, and because it is opposed to impurity.... Also, *tathatā* both exists and does not exist [i.e., is empty], because it is endowed with [both] qualities [of existence and emptiness].
>
> The nature which is dependent on another [*paratantra svabhāva*; i.e., phenomenal reality as the product of causes and conditions] means existence, because it is formed from conditions and because it lacks a nature of its own.... Also, it means nonexistence, because that which is created from conditions has no nature of its own.... It both exists and does not exist, because it is formed from conditions and has no nature of its own.[10]

Several important statements are made in this passage. First, the absolute is said to be existent or nonempty because it is immutable (or indestructible, which is the term used here). It is also empty because it is subject to conditions, and we thus have here another form of the statement made about the gold in the foregoing analogy. When he turns to phenomenal existence, Fa-tsang also says that it is both existent and empty; it is existent because it is a product of conditions, and it is empty because it has no nature of its own. Keeping in mind that Fa-tsang, like many Chinese Buddhists, used the terms "existence" and "nonexistence" interchangeably with the more orthodox "form" (*rūpa*) and "emptiness" respectively, his equations will look like this:

$$
\text{Absolute} \left\{ \begin{array}{l} \text{Immutability} = \text{existence} \\ \text{Obeys conditions} = \text{emptiness (nonexistence)} \end{array} \right.
$$

$$
\text{Phenomena} \left\{ \begin{array}{l} \text{Quasi-existence (conditionedness)} = \text{existence} \\ \text{Without a } svabhāva = \text{nonexistence (emptiness)} \end{array} \right.
$$

Of course, since the absolute expresses itself as the world of things, the two main categories above are simply two sides of the same thing, their "thingness" and their absoluteness, and it is obvious that no matter which aspect we examine, we find the same two qualities of existence and emptiness. Looked at from the standpoint of absoluteness, immutability is equated with existence and conditionedness is equated with emptiness. When we further examine the object from the standpoint of its phenomenality, its conditionedness is equated with existence, while its lack of self-nature (*svabhāva*) is equated with emptiness. Since the conditionedness of the absolute is none other than its appearance as conditioned existence, what is called emptiness from one point of view is called existence from the other. Likewise, the emptiness of phenomenal things is merely the "existence" of the immutable absolute. In this way, emptiness and existence are one and the same thing, a perfect reflection of the well-known statement from the *Prajñāpāramitā Sūtra* which says that form (existence) is emptiness and emptiness is form (*rūpam śūnyatā, śūnyataiva rūpam*). Here, once more, Fa-tsang is saying that the *real* existence of conditioned things is an immutable absolute. Primary in importance, however, is his use of the terms "existence" and "emptiness" in connection with the absolute and the phenomenal. If we can further determine how he understood these two terms, we can then better understand what he means by "immutability" and consequently how we may understand what Vairocana is.

Fortunately, there are many passages in Hua-yen literature which discuss existence and emptiness; actually, the whole of the literature deals with little else than these categories and their relationship. Like most Buddhist literature, Hua-yen texts are greatly concerned with the question of how, or in what manner, things exist. This is to be expected of a religion which is based on the assumption that the foremost problem confronting man in his existential plight is his inability to understand the nature of things, including himself. Therefore, most Buddhist literature eschews any discussion of the religious goal of emancipation and wisdom per se as ultimately incommunicable, and rather devotes its energies to an analysis of the phenomenal world. Hua-yen is remarkable in that more than other forms of Buddhism it attempts to give some idea of what existence is like in the eyes of those who are awakened, but in the course of this description, there is much talk of existence, or form, and emptiness.

One of the best sources for a study of Fa-tsang's understanding of these terms is his commentary on the famous *Heart Sūtra* (*Prajñāpāramitā-hṛdaya Sūtra*). As is well known by all students of Buddhism, this brief sutra, of about one printed page in its English translation, presents the gist or "heart" of the teachings of the vast *Prajñāpāramitā* literature: "form is emptiness and emptiness is form." Since this scripture is wholly concerned with the relationship between the two categories of form and emptiness, Fa-tsang's commentary on it will illuminate his own grasp of these terms, and this in turn will help us to understand what he means when he says that the immutable absolute is the true reality of phenomenal existence.

In commenting on the lines of the sutra which say, "O Śāriputra, form is not different from emptiness, emptiness is not different from form. Form is identical with emptiness and emptiness is identical with form. The same is true with regard to feelings, ideas, volition, and consciousness," Fa-tsang says that the passage is meant to dispel doubts and misunderstanding of some Buddhists concerning emptiness:

> The doubts [of the Hinayana] are as follows: "Our small vehicle sees that while the psycho-physical being exists, the constituents of personality [skandhas] are lacking in a self. What is the difference between this and the emptiness of dharmas?" We explain this by saying that your belief is that the absence of a self among the constituents of personality is called "emptiness of the person." It is not that each of the skandhas itself is empty. In your case, the skandhas are different from emptiness. Now we explain that the skandhas themselves are [each] empty of a self-essence [svabhāva], which is different from your position. Therefore, the sutra says that "Form is not different from emptiness," etc.
>
> Also, they doubt in this way: "According to our small vehicle, when one enters the state in which there is no more psycho-physical being [i.e., final nirvāṇa], mind and body are both terminated. How does this differ from [your doctrine of] 'emptiness is without form'?" The explanation is this: in your doctrine, form is not [in itself] empty, but only when form is destroyed is there then emptiness. This, however, is not the case. Form is identical with emptiness; it is not an emptiness which results from the destruction of form. Therefore, it is not at all the same [as what you teach].[11]

Further on, the same explanation is given to the fledgling Bodhisattva, whose understanding is still unripe; this time, however, a third point is added:

> The third doubt [entertained by the Bodhisattva] is that he believes that emptiness is an entity. Now [the sutra] shows that emptiness is identical with form. One should not try to seize emptiness with [the notion of] emptiness.[12]

Several conclusions about Fa-tsang's grasp of the emptiness doctrine can be made on the basis of these passages. First, in keeping with general Mahayana doctrine, Fa-tsang knew that emptiness refers not to just the absence of a central self or substance around which the five *skandhas* are organized (i.e., *pudgala śūnyatā*), but that it means that each of the five *skandhas* is in itself empty of a *svabhāva* (*dharma śūnyatā*). Thus, for instance, *rūpa*, or matter, has no substance, nor has feeling, and so on. The non-Mahayana forms of Buddhism believed that while there was no inner self which possessed and used the psycho-physical organism, the organism itself as the five *skandhas* was a real thing. Now Fa-tsang, a good Mahayanist and a good student of *Śūnyavāda* doctrine, shows that each of the *skandhas* is, as well, empty of a self or substance. Second, he was well aware that emptiness does not refer merely to the absence or annihilation of something. In other words, he did not make the naive mistake of thinking that to say that something was empty meant that it was a nonentity. Emptiness is not something which occurs when a thing vanishes but is said of things which are there, just as to say that my pocket is empty does not mean I have no pocket, but rather means that there is a pocket which has nothing in it. Again, Fa-tsang appeals to the sutra, which says that form and emptiness are literally identical. Finally, in clearing up the problem of the Bodhisattva, Fa-tsang makes the extremely important point that emptiness is *not a thing* and that the Bodhisattva should not make the mistake of reifying emptiness and thus making it just one more thing, albeit perhaps a more exalted thing. As far back as Seng-chao, Chinese Buddhists knew that emptiness was not merely a more spiritual thing among lesser things, and thus was not some noumenous entity within phenomenal entities.[13] *Form itself is emptiness.*

So far, Fa-tsang's views appear to be well within the older orthodox Mahayana tradition. Later on, in the same commentary, he continues his discussion of existence and emptiness.

> First, they are opposed to each other. A passage a little further on [in the sutra] says "in emptiness there is no form," because emptiness injures form. In the same way, it can be said that "in form there is no emptiness," because form opposes emptiness. The reason for this is that even though they always exist together, they also nevertheless destroy each other. Second, they are not mutually opposing. This means that since form is illusory form, form cannot obstruct emptiness. Because emptiness is true emptiness [and not the emptiness of annihilation or absence], it does not obstruct illusory form. If it did obstruct form, it would be emptiness as annihilation and therefore not real emptiness. If [form] really obstructed emptiness, then it would be real form, not illusory form. Third, they are mutually creative. That is, if

this illusory form were to exhibit an essence, then it would not be empty, and therefore could not become illusory form. The *Pañcaviṁśatisāhasrikā-prajñāpāramitā Sūtra* says, "If all *dharmas* are not empty, there can be no religious practices, no religious goal," etc. According to the *Mādhyamika-kārikās* [by Nāgārjuna], "Because there is the principle of emptiness, all *dharmas* are able to be formed."[14]

Fa-tsang makes the following points in this passage: (1) To say that *dharmas* are empty is to deny the ultimacy and self-existence of the *dharmas*. Accordingly, to speak of form is to deny emptiness, in the sense that to see only form is to overlook its emptiness. Even though the two are never really found apart, to see the one aspect of things only is to be oblivious to the other. (2) The two aspects do not really negate each other. Real emptiness does not nullify or abolish form because emptiness is not to be construed as utter nonbeing. At the same time, form cannot nullify emptiness because it is lacking in ultimate reality. On the contrary, things exist as things only by virtue of their true emptiness. (3) Form and emptiness are mutually creative. If things were not empty of a substance or essence, they could not exist even for a second; conversely, without things, there can be no emptiness. This is not hard to understand if it is remembered that emptiness refers only to the mode of being of existents. Fa-tsang quotes the *Prajñāpāramitā* literature in support of this last point, as well as Nāgārjuna's treatise, which is a systematic discussion of these same concepts.[15] The Buddhist axiom at the base of this latter statement is that if an entity possesses a *svabhāva*, which by definition is eternal and immutable, then that entity is not capable of any modification. If a *dharma* such as the Buddhist *mārga* had a *svabhāva* and thus existed absolutely independent of all conditions, there could never be any change in the aspirant either for better or worse. However, since the *dharma*-entity is empty, meaning existing only in interdependence with other factors, then conditions can effect a modification in that entity. Thus it is a orthodox for Fa-tsang to say that things can only exist because they are empty. To repeat, emptiness cannot exist apart from entities, since emptiness is a relationship between entities: they create each other, are thoroughly interfused, and in fact are one and the same thing.

Fa-tsang concludes the above passage with the following comment: "Even though this true emptiness is the same as form [and other *dharmas*], still, form arises from conditions. True emptiness does not create form. In accordance with conditions, [form] perishes. True emptiness does not extinguish [form]."[16] Thus although form and emptiness are thoroughly mixed and in a real sense mutually creative, form is not produced from emptiness nor does it perish from its operation. Emptiness, which is the *law* of interdependent origination, should not be conceived as an ontologically prior entity or being out of which things originate and through the operation of which they cease to be. However, at the same time, even though emptiness does not exist apart from entities, the appearance and disappearance of these entities does not affect the law of inter-dependent existence, nor, in sentient beings, does merit or demerit have any effect on emptiness. It is not, says Fa-tsang, soiled in its form of *samsāra*, nor is it purified when the being eliminates moral and intellectual faults (*kleśa*).[17]

What is particularly significant in all these discussions of emptiness and existence in Fa-tsang's writings is that he seems to have had an accurate and deep under-standing of the Indian Buddhist concept of emptiness as being synonymous with the teaching of interdependent origination, *pratītyasamutpāda*. Hence he was aware of the statement and the consequences of the statement made by Nāgārjuna in his *kārikās*: "It is declared that interdependent origination is emptiness" (*Kārikās* 24:18). Nowhere in these passages, or in any other, is there any evidence that Fa-tsang had an incorrect understanding of the Indian teaching. Another passage from Fa-tsang's writings, the "Tranquillity and Insight of the Five Doctrines of Buddhism," indicates this beyond any question:

> All *dharmas* without exception are characterized by emptiness. . . . First, they are contemplated as being birthless. Second, they are contemplated as being markless [i.e., *animitta*]. "Contemplated as being birthless" means that *dharmas* have no nature of their own [i.e., *svabhāva*]. They are mutually causative and come into existence in this manner. In their birth, they do not exist in reality, and so they are empty. They are as empty and nonexistent as anything can be. Therefore, they are said to be birthless. A sutra says, "They are conditioned and therefore exist; they are without a nature of their own and therefore are empty." This means that being without a nature of its own is identical with being conditioned. Being conditioned is identical with being without a nature of its own. The *Mādhyamika-kārikās* say, "All *dharmas* are formed as a result of existence and emptiness."[18]

Here, Fa-tsang uses the technical term *dharma* to mean "an entity," and it corre-sponds to his use of the term "existence" and to the "form" of the *Heart Sūtra* (although technically form is merely one of many *dharmas*). He says of a *dharma*: (1) it has no *svabhāva*, (2) it comes into existence (and passes out of existence) as a result of conditions, and (3) its existence consists of its being formed from conditions, and its emptiness lies in its being utterly lacking in a *svabhāva*. The upshot of this discussion, consequently, is that emptiness and existence (or *dharmas*, entities, or form) are literally identical, because existing purely as a result of conditions and being without an independent existence (empty) are one and the same, a fundamental point in Buddhist thought. Thus, when there are things, there is emptiness, and when there is emptiness, there are empty things. We need not look for emptiness outside the world of phenomenal entities.[19]

Therefore, since form is identical with emptiness, the *Vimalakīrti Sūtra*, a vastly influential Mahayana scripture, says, "Beings are identical with *nirvāṇa* and do not have to enter *nirvāṇa* again."[20] At the same time, since emptiness is identical with form, the *Sūtra on Neither Increase Nor Decrease* can say, "The Dharma-body of the *Tathāgata* transmigrating among the five forms of sentient existence is called 'sentient beings.' "[21] In other words, all things are the body of Vairocana.

It is now time to return to the question raised at the beginning of this chapter: Who, or What, is Vairocana? We know that the emptiness of phenomenal reality, which is conceived by Buddhists to be the absolute, and anthropomorphized in the form of Vairocana, is the interdependent, or intercausal, mode by which things come into existence, exist, and cease to exist. It would already seem evident, then, that "Vairocana" is merely a name given to the law of interdependent origination or interdependent existence. Far from being a substance or metaphysical essence, it is the law which utterly denies the existence of such an entity. Then in what sense are we to understand Vairocana as immutable? Certainly not as stasis, since interdependent existence is a dynamic process beyond comprehension. It is, in fact, this very dynamic process itself which is immutable; i.e., it is the *immutability of mutability*, the law which determines that every single particle of the universe constantly changes due to the existence of conditions about it. It may seem strange to speak of the immutability of mutability, but for the Buddhist, who subjects experience to the most thoroughgoing, ruthless positivistic scrutiny, there is nothing in experience which seems to mitigate a perpetual cosmic change. It is the transcendental, "ever-thus" character of interdependence which is the immutability of Vairocana, or ascribed to Vairocana. On the other hand, the conditionedness of the absolute does not imply its prior existence or the emanation serially of the universe of entities from its own substance. It means simply that the emptiness or nonexistence which is the absolute is immanent in phenomena and never found apart from them. In what sense emptiness constitutes the ground of these entities, and in what sense it can be said that it *becomes* entities, and that it is subject to conditions, can be clarified if we digress for a moment in the area of general Buddhist teachings concerning man's problems.

According to Mahayana Buddhism, the problem for human beings begins with the habit of superimposing constructs of a purely subjective nature upon the immediacy of concrete experience,[22] thus imposing categories of a valuative nature upon an experience which does not intrinsically possess these values.

Moreover, the division of the unity of experience itself into fragments must be seen as the outcome of a desire to manipulate experience for one's own selfish purposes. Thus according to Hua-yen, which is certainly well within the tradition of Mahayana Buddhism, the essential unity of the *dharma-dhātu* of identity and interdependence becomes, for all of us, divided into pieces, these pieces are invested with imaginary substances which seem to give them an aura of ultimacy, and then these pieces are arranged in a hierarchy of good and bad. Conversely, liberation, *mokṣa*, is achieved through the eradication of this divisive, categorizing, and evaluative habit. This is the point of the emptiness doctrine, which attempts to make people see that reality does not correspond with our concepts of it. Thus the absolute becomes conditioned in the sense that the real manner of being of phenomenal existence is conditioned by our ignorance (*avidyā*), so that rather than appearing as itself, as emptiness, it appears in the ignorant manner discussed above. (There is another sense in which the absolute is conditioned, which will be mentioned further on.) In Buddhist terms, *tathatā*, the "thusness" quality of things seen as they really are, becomes subjected to false imaginings (*vikalpa*). The world as it exists for most of us is thus in a very real sense born of ignorance and desire.

Immutability may be considered to be the transcendental aspect of the absolute, while conditionedness may be regarded as its immanent aspect. Although it may seem that the absolute cannot be both transcendental and immanent, it is in fact both. The word "transcendental" only seems to conflict with the immanence of the absolute, but this is because we who were raised in the Western tradition usually conceive of the transcendental nature of the absolute as raising it beyond the world of nature, so that there is a true gulf, forever unremovable, between the absolute and the phenomenal or relative. The Western god does not abide in his creation, and it is a heresy to locate him in it. He may be involved in it in some sense, but he is apart from it in the same way that a great king dwells apart from his subjects. The very idea of immanence raises the specter of that pantheism which is so abhorred by the great Western monotheistic religions, and which they regard as the mark of a "lower" religion. However, "transcendental" can be used in another sense besides the spatial one; it can indicate that "plus-quality" which raises the absolute above the relative in terms of value, without removing it actually from the relative itself. This is particularly appropriate for Vairocana, who is the emptiness of things, for, as we have seen, since emptiness refers to the relational mode of entities, it cannot ever exist apart from the things which we say are empty and therefore must be immanent in a most integral manner. However, it is precisely this emptiness, the face of Vairocana, hidden to empirical investigation, which is revealed in the Buddhist enlightenment with a concomitant spiritualizing and saving effect on the devotee. It is the revelation of this emptiness as a "plus-quality" in things, elevating them above the brute materiality and facticity of mere things, and at the same time effecting a profound inner transformation in the individual, which we may recognize as the transcendental quality of the absolute. Therefore, there is really no inconsistency in referring to Vairocana as both transcendental and immanent. He is indeed both. We may return again briefly to the pregnant assertion of the *Heart Sūtra*, which says "form is emptiness, and emptiness is form." Because form is empty, there is a transcendental "plus-quality" in phenomenal existence which is ultimately knowable if one can but see clearly and wholly. At the same time, because emptiness is form, we may search for this quality in phenomenal existence itself, for it can be discovered nowhere else. In the end, this means nothing more—difficult as it is to truly see and then act accordingly—than that things exist only in an interdependent manner.

"Vairocana," then, is a mere sound, a symbol for the manner in which things exist, and therefore there is no point in praying to Vairocana, loving him, fearing him, asking for favors, and so on. One cannot ask the law of gravity to give one some special favor or to relax its inexorable work for a moment. It may seem peculiar to speak of a law in such a manner as Buddhists do of Vairocana, or to anthropomorphize this law as a being named Vairocana, but then we are only quarreling with the human habits of language, not with the meaning of the word. Were it not for habit, Buddhists would undoubtedly be willing to call the law something else—"God," for instance—since words are not important as long as we know what they mean. But, having said this, another doubt may arise; if Vairocana is the same as emptiness, and if emptiness is the same as interdependence, is the Buddhist attitude toward Vairocana nothing but a sophisticated nature worship? Moreover, is not this nature worship merely estheticism raised ten degrees, and not religion at all? Certainly the esthetic element is not missing from the Hua-yen attitude toward the natural world, but it goes beyond estheticism. As has been mentioned before, the Hua-yen vision is not the vision of the common man, trapped in greed, hatred, and delusion. It is the vision of Buddhas, those rare individuals who have destroyed these impulses in themselves and who thus no longer are subject to the sorrow, anxiety, and turmoil that torment others. Thus the vision of things as described by Hua-yen is much more than the ecstatic appreciation of nature in its beauty and awesomeness; it comes only with the most cataclysmic spiritual and psychological transformation of the individual. More than this, it accompanies a radical reorientation in one's dealings with other people and all other things living and nonliving. It is said that enlightenment ideally is the beginning of a career of selfless giving and unconditional compassion for all that exists. Can this be construed as mere nature worship?

It may be thought that the object of worship in Hua-yen—if we can use that word—is a rather thin abstraction, after all, perhaps somewhat similar in kind to the second law of thermodynamics or the law of gravity. Yet it is indeed true that in Buddhism in general, the object of devotion is law, the Dharma. Chinese Buddhists habitually used the terms "Tao" and *li*, the first meaning the "Way" in which things occurred naturally, the second having the original meaning of "pattern," meaning the pattern found throughout nature. But a Buddha is more than the mere personification of an abstract law; there have been flesh and blood Buddhas in the world from time to time. Earlier it was said that the absolute is conditioned in the sense that man's ignorance as condition causes the absolute to appear as "things," but there is another sense also in which it can be said that the absolute is conditioned. The model for this event has been established by the historical founder of Buddhism, Śākyamuni. His biographies show him as being motivated to leave the life of worldly self-indulgence and going forth to seek the truth because he was overcome with pity for the suffering of mankind. Thus his own enlightenment, which is the actualization or realization of the law within himself, must be seen as conditioned by the suffering and wailing of living beings. Put in another way, the absolute has appeared in the world of time and space because of conditions, and these conditions are those of ignorance and suffering. When the Buddhist of later times made his Bodhisattva vows to help all sentient beings to become free and then proceeded to carry out the practices which culminated in his own enlightenment, he only reenacted the event which occurred in the person of Śākyamuni, when the absolute, under the strong pull of overwhelming conditions, took on form. Indeed, it is because of this event that Buddhists can identify the emptiness which lies at the root of existence with compassion.

Finally, it needs to be said that the vision of Vairocana is this same realization of Vairocana within oneself, so that seeing and being become identical. Another way of saying this is that the dawning of *prajñā*, by which one sees the emptiness of things, is an act of absolute encompassing whereby one's own boundaries expand to include everything. Thus to see emptiness is to become emptiness, or, better, to become empty is to see emptiness. The *Avataṁsaka Sūtra* succinctly and clearly says what I have tried to clarify in many pages:

> Clearly know that all *dharmas*
> Are without any self-essence at all;

To understand the nature of *dharmas* in this way
Is to see Vairocana.[23]

The whole of existence is thus the body of Vairocana, for what is there that is not empty? Understood in this way, and only in this way, Hua-yen can be said to teach pan-Buddhism.[24]

8

Living in the Net of Indra

It is time now, in this final chapter, to remind the reader of a point made much earlier in this book. Primarily, Buddhism is praxis, something that one does. Although elements such as having faith, possessing a warm feeling about the religion, and adhering to certain credal formulas are not absent from Buddhism, it may safely be said that these things are not in themselves enough. Likewise, there is a lot of "philosophy" in Buddhism, in the form of logic, cosmology, and epistemology, but to be a Buddhist entails much more than having a certain philosophy of existence. One must make the philosophy a lived reality, so that systems of thought such as Hua-yen must give rise to a particular mode of activity. Otherwise, the believer is merely indulging in intellectual fun, and Buddhism would claim that the problem of life is too pressing to waste in fruitless mind-games.

Faith, attitudes, credal purity, and the like, are not without value, but in themselves they are insufficient for spiritual freedom. They may help in some way to make the long journey to infinite light, but the journey itself is a series of acts of a certain kind, including some glimpse, however partial and imperfect, of the light itself. Thus the Bodhisattva who begins to wend his way down the eons must do more than believe in his religion, and he must do more than gain an understanding of the nature of existence through a study of philosophical texts; he must act as if the Hua-yen vision were an indubitable reality. Buddhism therefore places a great amount of stress on meditation and the ethical life which is the outflow of this meditation, for both are at once practical means of realizing the Hua-yen *dharma-dhātu* and an acting out of the reality of that vision. The function of Hua-yen thought, as was remarked earlier, is to be a lure which attracts the aspirant to the practice which will presumably culminate in an existential, or experiential, validation of what was before only theory. At the same time, it guides the aspirant in actual interrelationships, serving as a kind of template by means of which the individual may gauge the extent to which his actions conform to the reality of identity and interdependence.

Needless to say, Hua-yen did not invent Buddhist ethics, nor did it invent the overall picture of the Bodhisattva's path with its many stages of development. This *mārga* scheme was already in existence when Hua-yen arose. What it did do in its attempt to comprehend the whole of Buddhism within one grand synthesis was to supply a more thorough rationale for the Bodhisattva's path than had been achieved before the arising of Hua-yen. In doing this, it laid a basis for ethical life and for various important Buddhist concepts which was ambitious in its attempt and satisfying in its achievement.

This chapter concentrates on several key items in the inventory of Buddhist thought and practice. First, there is the path of the Bodhisattva, conceived by Hua-yen as stretching over fifty-three stages and countless *kalpas*. What is that path, and what is the relationship between the various stages? Second, since the path is for the purpose of enlightenment, when does this enlightenment occur? Is this enlightenment something one achieves in a flash, or does it come to the aspirant gradually, over a long period of time? Third, and closely related to the previous question, whose enlightenment is it when the aspirant is enlightened? Is it his alone, or do all share in it in some manner? A corollary of this is the question of the relationship of any one individual's ignorance or nonenlightenment (*avidyā*) to other beings. Fourth, and finally, a rather extensive question: Granted that the picture of existence as portrayed by Hua-yen is a true picture, how should I conduct myself in my relationship with the infinity that is the other? Why should I bother to seek enlightenment at all? Is there any moral imperative, even implicit, in Hua-yen which demands that I make this search? Most important, what is the relationship between the goal sought by the aspirant and the ethical stance which he takes? This chapter will investigate these, as well as some ancillary matters, in the light of the portrait of the *dharma-dhātu* so painstakingly created by Fa-tsang and his tradition.

The Bodhisattva *mārga* is conceived as being a very long, heroic endeavor, covering many lifetimes, marked in each life by the total commitment of the Bodhisattva to emancipate all beings even at the expense of his own life. But in order to do this, he must take pains never to actually reach the final stage in his career, perfect enlightenment, for were he to finally reach the fifty-third stage he would cease forever to be reborn in the destinies of woe, and as a consequence, he would not have the opportunity to work for the good of all beings. According to Fa-tsang, he prevents this by deliberately retaining some of the moral and intellectual faults (*kleśa*) which will bind him to rebirth, thus enabling him to be perpetually reborn in the evil paths in order to aid suffering beings.[1] Since presumably there will always be beings who need help, the Bodhisattva's career is endless, and of course this means that he is forever shut off from the goal which he could have if he wished. Such is the heroic, compassionate career of the Bodhisattva. However, there is a paradox here, and it has been noted in the *Laṅkāvatāra Sūtra*; in deliberately refusing the final goal of the highest, perfect enlightenment, which comes at the fifty-third stage, the Bodhisattva in fact acquires the *only real enlightenment*, which is nothing but the renunciation of personal desires so complete that even the highest good of *nirvāṇa* is tossed away as if it were the merest trifle.[2] The *Saddharmapuṇḍarīka Sūtra* tells us that even the Buddha himself has not finished his Bodhisattva work, though he has trained for incalculable eons.[3]

Admittedly this is a grand concept, and it is obviously one which places almost unrealistic demands on the aspirant, who is, after all, a human being, and a human being who lives with other beings who probably do not share his exalted view of things. For what this commitment means in concrete terms is that even before he is a perfect Buddha, the Bodhisattva must begin to follow the vocation of a Buddha. That is, he must begin his mission of emancipating all beings, even at the cost of his own life, at exactly the point in his career where he presently finds himself. According to the Japanese Zen master Dōgen, the question which all Buddhas ask is, "How can I cause beings to enter the supreme Way and speedily perfect Buddha bodies?,"[4] because a Buddha's life is nothing but the cosmic task of making all beings over into Buddhas. The Bodhisattva must likewise ask the same question at all stages of development, even at the very beginning of his mission, for he cannot wait until he has acquired the rare and special abilities of a perfect Buddha.

The basis of this idea can be found in several places. First, there are the *exempla* of the *jātakas*, the previous lives of the man who became the founder of Buddhism. In these stories we see that even though the being who was ultimately to become a Buddha had not yet become one, these previous lives were all marked by a selflessness and compassionate action which were to culminate in perfection. The insight and compassion which are the "two wings of Buddhahood" were thus abundantly evident in an individual who was still far from perfection. Second, there is a kind of logic at the root of this activity. That is, the perfection of Buddhahood, defined as absolute egolessness and compassion, can hardly be achieved by someone who selfishly and egotistically strives for his own private perfection. This inner contradiction of selfishly seeking selflessness thus leads to a new orientation. The Bodhisattva abandons his own ultimate reward and dedicates his life, and all future lives, to the emancipation of every last living being. But this training in insight and compassion to which he commits himself is itself the very life-activity of a Buddha. Here too is a paradox, for in a Buddhist version of "one hand washing another," as the Bodhisattva strives ceaselessly to benefit others, he is also benefiting himself all the time.[5] In a spiraling dialectical movement which traverses the eons, the Bodhisattva benefits others; this benefit increases his own insight and compassion, and this in turn better equips him to benefit other beings. Thus to help others is really to help oneself; to help oneself is to help others. The ultimate good of *nirvāṇa* is not really lost sight of in the eons of selfless giving to others, and while practically speaking the Bodhisattva's mission will never end, in theory he will enter final *nirvāṇa* side by side with the last being. In time, say the scriptures, every living thing, even the grass, will enter the unspeakable bliss of *nirvāṇa*. Were it otherwise, it would not be the Dharma.

But logic and scriptural testimony aside, what reason is there for believing that Buddha activity is present in all stages of the *mārga*, not excluding the very early stage of the beginner? The basis is, of course, the truth of emptiness, *śūnyatā*. The fifty-three stages of the Bodhisattva are as empty as any other thing, which is to say that any stage, including the stage of Buddhahood, possesses only a contingent existence. Their identity, that is, is precisely their interdependent being. According to Fa-tsang,

> If one stage is acquired, all stages are acquired, because [each stage] possesses the six characteristics [of universality and particularity, etc.], because of the infinite interrelationship of primary and secondary, because of mutual interpenetration, because of mutual identity, and because of mutual inter-fusion. The *Avataṁsaka Sūtra* says, "One stage includes the qualities of all stages throughout." Therefore, what is meant here is the acquisition of all stages as well as the stage of Buddhahood as soon as one has reached that part [of the path] which is called "superior progress," which is the perfection of faith.

He then concludes,

> Because all stages including the stage of Buddhahood are identical, then cause and effect are not different, and beginning and end interpenetrate. *On each stage, one is thus both a Bodhisattva and a Buddha.* [My emphasis][6]

Thus, according to Fa-tsang, when one reaches that stage of development which is the perfection of the stage of faith, one is both a Bodhisattva and a Buddha, and, of course, the same dual role is played at each of the following forty-three stages. The causal stage of faith and the resultant stage of perfect Buddhahood interpenetrate, are identical, are mutually dependent, and equally empty. For the details of this situation, the reader may recall the arguments in Chapter 6 on the analogy of the building. In essence, the situation is this: if the stage of faith is truly a causal stage, there must, by implication, be a resultant stage, which is Buddhahood, because it is the result which makes the cause a cause. The eventual attainment of the result in fact proves that the stage of faith was causal in nature. In the analogy of the building, we have a parallel case, where the part-rafter can only be a rafter when the whole building is present, making the rafter a rafter. If this seems to be a specious argument, it must be remembered that any part, according to Hua-yen, is only a part due to the fact that the whole makes it a part. Therefore, the whole path, including Buddhahood, must be present during the first stage of development.

Now, such a view naturally leads to the corollary view of the Bodhisattva, even in the early stage of faith, as already endowed with the powers and majesty of full Buddhahood. Fa-tsang praises the Bodhisattva extravagantly:

> From the [point of development of] perfection of faith and the attainment of the stages onward, the activities of the Bodhisattva which have come into being fill up the entire *dharma-dhātu*. According to the [*Avataṁsaka*] sutra, for instance, "With one hand he can cover the immense trichiliocosm. The ritual implements which he holds in his hands are as extensive as space and the *dharma-dhātu*. He honors countless Buddhas simultaneously, performs all the activities of a Buddha, and his benefit to living beings is inexpressible."[7]

With forty-three stages left to traverse, the Bodhisattva is already performing the miracles of a Buddha.

Here, the question may easily arise as to why the Bodhisattva should bother with the remaining forty-three stages, since even as a neophyte the activities of Buddhahood are present. Fa-tsang admits that the later stages, posterior to faith, are necessary and that indeed the Bodhisattva cannot stop his training after faith is ripe. According to the Treatise, the remaining stages are taught because "they are the 'all' which are included in the first. These later stages are the same as the first [in including all]."[8] This rather cryptic answer need not trouble us if we keep firmly in mind the doctrine of interdependent being. While the later stages are in some sense present in the first stage, nevertheless, the first stage is only a first stage relative to the second, third, and so on. If those later stages are not patiently perfected also, the first stage was not really a first stage at all. In fact, simultaneity and sequence are both realities, just as in the general picture given by Hua-yen, all things are simultaneously particular and universal, individuals but also the totality.

> Previous and later being mutually inclusive [i.e., interpenetrating] and completely interfused without obstacle, they are different from [the stages in] the three vehicles. . . . Still, the stages are not disturbed, and yet they are identical; and this identity is not disturbed, but there still remains always a sequence. Therefore the two concepts are mutually inclusive, with no contradiction between them.[9]

Consequently, while the Bodhisattva must perfect each of the stages in order, on each stage all the qualities of the remaining stages, including Buddhahood, are present.

I believe that in this treatment of the stages, there is another issue at stake, however muted it may be. This is the very important doctrine of "Buddha-nature." It will be recalled that in an earlier quotation in this chapter, Fa-tsang spoke of a situation in which "cause and effect are not different, and beginning and end interpenetrate." Now, if the effect or fruit of the Bodhisattva's causal practices is Buddhahood, and if cause and effect are identical, Fa-tsang's comment is tantamount to saying that the causal state must be Buddha-result itself. This is a thorough mixing of cause and effect, because what is conventionally considered to be the fruit of a long sequence of acts is now said to be that which is present right from the very beginning and, indeed, that which is performing the causal acts. But in a universe which is claimed to be the body of Vairocana, it should not be surprising that Buddha-nature is not only completely pervasive spatially but is temporally omnipresent as well. This is not, in Chinese Buddhism, an unorthodox doctrine, because it simply deals in a different manner with the older, common distinction of "intrinsic enlightenment" and "acquired enlightenment."[10] According to this doctrine, all beings are endowed with intrinsic enlightenment from the beginning, and the existential realization of this true nature occurs when the intrinsic enlightenment is "nourished" by acquired enlightenment, the training of the stages of the Bodhisattva. A common metaphor for this is that of the seed which becomes a sprout when it has been moistened by the rain. This indicates a situation in which it is really the intrinsic enlightenment, or fundamental Buddha-nature, which is acting as an impetus to training, and indeed which is acting through the individual in a process of self-realization.

Something else is involved also, and that is the well-known and troublesome doctrine of "sudden enlightenment." As we see this concept developed by such men as Hui-neng, the Japanese Sōtō Zen master Dōgen, and others, it becomes evident that the issue over sudden enlightenment as opposed to gradual enlightenment had little or nothing to do with the question of the speed with which the enlightenment event occurred. All schools of Buddhism agreed that the enlightenment event was of necessity a sudden one. Rather, the question centered around the issue of whether enlightenment had to be preceded by a progressive course of moral improvement. The "suddenists" such as Hui-neng denied the necessity of prior training, and their basis for this was the conviction that beings are already enlightened, albeit ignorant of their enlightenment. That is, they were endowed with intrinsic enlightenment. In the writings of Hui-neng and Dōgen, then, there is a strong denial of meditation and ethics as means to the end which is enlightenment; instead, we find that training is that which merely manifests, or draws out, that which one already is in theory.[11] Therefore, training is not at all negated by the suddenists, including the Hua-yen masters, who also considered themselves to be suddenists. This idea, which is one of the prominent features of Sino-Japanese Buddhism, is here reflected in the totalistic arguments of Hua-yen, where we also see that the Bodhisattva, at the dawn of his career, carries out the compassionate, insightful deeds of the Buddha, but must also continue his training throughout the fifty-three stages if that Buddha activity is to be strengthened and deepened.

When Fa-tsang says that cause and effect are the same, he is perhaps reflecting some of the creative intellectual ferment that was taking place during the Sui-T'ang period, particularly with regard to the question of the relationship between the absolute and relative (*li* and *shih*), and with regard to the question of whether a person had to wait several eons in order to become a Buddha, a question of great importance to Chinese Buddhists.[12] The conclusion was that the Buddha seed is present right from the beginning, requiring only the nourishment of practice in order to sprout, flourish, and bloom. It is really this intrinsic Buddha-nature which acts to realize itself, not the individual. That is, Buddhahood is its own cause. Such an idea, so pregnant with possibilities for the career of the Bodhisattva, eventually culminated, in fact, in the perceptive and profoundly religious observation of Dōgen, who said that "no ordinary beings ever became Buddhas; only Buddhas become Buddhas."[13] This can only be a world in which the Buddha realizes himself in and through beings in an act of cosmic, eternal self-limitation.

The Bodhisattva cannot, and need not, wait through the eons in order to eventually equip himself to perform the compassionate deeds of a Buddha. He can and must begin early in his course of training to act as if he were a Buddha. While in the beginning his career will be marked by success and failure, continual training will result in the development of his abilities. It may seem, as I have said, a great burden to lay on the neophyte Bodhisattva, but we must bear in mind that the Mahayana conception of the Bodhisattva is a truly exalted one. The real Bodhisattva (and not the "Bodhisattva in name only") is that individual who has reached a crucial turning point in his career, when he can, in all sincerity and with an absolute commitment, make a vow to emancipate all living beings before he is emancipated himself. The figure of Amida, in Japanese Pure Land Buddhism, is perhaps the epitome of this ideal, along with his "spiritual son," Kannon. If the aspirant cannot make this vow, he is not a Bodhisattva.[14]

It can be seen, then, that the Hua-yen tradition offers its own kind of reasons as to why Buddha activity is present in all phases of Bodhisattva activity. Implicit is the understanding that Buddha-nature is a reality even in the "green" Bodhisattva, and that his arduous training will make this nature a reality which will illuminate his experience and increasingly give power and direction to his acts. As Hua-yen sees the situation, this activity is possible because the universe is one of identity and interdependence.

We might pause here to make a brief summary of the Bodhisattva's career. At the outset of this career, he makes a vow in utter seriousness to postpone his own enlightenment until the day when all other beings, even the grass, enter the supreme bliss of *nirvāṇa*. At best, this dooms the Bodhisattva to enter the blazing heat of *saṃsāra* over and over again, throughout countless lifetimes, until he can enter the cool peace of *nirvāṇa* simultaneously with the last poor soul. At the worst, he will never reach his ideal goal, for viewed realistically, there will always be a considerable pool of unemancipated beings in need of ferrying across. These acts, which are of the nature of *prajñā*-insight and compassion (*karuṇā*), which are the very essence of Buddhahood, must not wait upon the Bodhisattva's achievement of ultimate enlightenment but must begin even at that point in his training when the Bodhisattva makes his great vow. Thus, while he unflaggingly pursues the life of the Bodhisattva in life after life, in all the destinies, from the purgatories up through the *deva* realms, at each of the fifty-three stages he must do the work of a Buddha. Dōgen, five centuries after the time of Fa-tsang, comments on this dual role:

> That which we call the ultimate is Buddhahood, or *bodhi*. If the highest, perfect enlightenment [*anuttara samyak sambodhi*] and this first arousal of the thought of enlightenment are compared, it is like the world-fire at the end of the eon compared with a firefly. And yet, having acknowledged this, if one arouses this enlightenment-thought of ferrying across all others to the other shore even though oneself has not yet been ferried across, there is no difference between the two.[15]

Not very many Buddhists make this ultimate commitment, just as the *imitatio Christi* is rather uncommon even among those who believe they are true Christians. If we ask why anyone would take upon himself this seemingly impossible burden, the answer must be that upon rare occasions, an individual appears who possesses such a profoundly religious spirit that he cannot conceive of accepting a reward which excludes even one of his suffering fellow beings. For him, it must be all or nothing, and if all beings do not enter the gate along with him, then, like Dharmākara in the *Large Sukhāvatī-vyūha Sūtra*, he will never accept the prize which is rightfully his. There is a touching story told in Hindu literature of a man who died and went to reap his reward in one of those Hindu heavens where the delights are beyond the imagination of men. He was accompanied by his beloved and faithful dog. When he reached the entrance of the heaven, he was stopped and told that only human beings could enter heaven. He thereupon told the gatekeeper that he would not enter heaven alone, for he could never leave behind the dog who had been so faithful a companion in life. Both man and dog were then allowed to enter into the heaven, for it developed that this was just a final test to determine whether the man really deserved to enjoy the delights of heaven. The question is, can we really forget the rest of that life of which we are part, turn our backs on the sighs and moans of living creatures, and greedily accept a prize, however holy and transcendent, which others cannot also enjoy? The Bodhisattva's answer is "No." The Bodhisattva might add, using the words of Jesus, "Truly I say to you, I shall be with you, even to the end of time."

Hua-yen Buddhism sees such a commitment as a necessary corollary of a universe which is a single organic body, one living Buddha body. If the Hua-yen vision of being contains any validity at all, then what touches one part of that body must touch the whole body. Because the whole web is shaken when one strand is touched, the whole of existence is somehow affected by the progress of the Bodhisattva. For the same reason, in a way which may elude those of us who are too engrossed in mundane matters of getting and spending, the ignorance, hatred, and desire which poison any one man's life must also poison the whole of existence. This being the case, any light which illuminates and transforms the existence of one person also helps to illuminate and transform the life of an Eskimo in northern Alaska, and by the same token, my own ignorance is also the ignorance of the nomad in the Kalahari Desert. Am I not the poorer because one man decided that six million Jews should be murdered? Likewise, because Bodhidharma sat in meditation, facing a cave wall for nine years, am I not the better? Who truly knows the outer limits of the radiating *karma* of any one man? Perhaps to pluck a flower is indeed to make a star in Orion tremble to its molten core. Only a Buddha really knows.

Not only is the reality of identity and interdependence the basis for Bodhisattva activity, but it also acts as a moral imperative, leaving the truly moral being with no option but to act in accordance with this reality. For if my own existence is unthinkable apart from the existence of this infinite other, and if my own actions touch these beings in some manner, then I must have an obligation to act in such a way that all benefit from the acts. I may, of course, choose otherwise, but then I am not acting in a fundamentally ethical manner, nor, of course, am I making any progress in my own development. But insight teaches me that my choices do indeed touch others, and in a manner unsuspected by Sartre, I choose for all when I choose for myself. It even reaches beyond the human, so that if I throw away a paper drinking cup, I can almost hear the reverberations of a falling tree in Michigan. If I choose the way of common men, I choose that all partake of some share of darkness and rage; if, on the contrary, I choose the way of light, I choose that all be bathed in light. If, as Hua-yen claims, all things are bound inextricably together in community, then what I will, will be the lot of all. Consequently, if I have the least shred of concern for my own spiritual progress, I must care—really care—for the spiritual growth of even the grass. We rise or fall together, like yucca plants and yucca moths. We are one body.

The Hua-yen tradition has found the answer to the nature of the Bodhisattva's career in the fact of a universe of identity and interdependence. The Bodhisattva cannot make a selfish, brash assault on the citadel of *nirvāṇa* because he knows he is not alone and that no one can enter alone. He must, therefore, find his own ultimate good in the good of the other. He is a sympathetic being in the same way that a string on a violin is sympathetic; when the other strings vibrate, it vibrates, and when it vibrates, so do the others. This is, admittedly, not the warm, melting sympathy known in human emotions, but a sympathy which is akin to the insight into emptiness itself. This may be said unequivocally; this sympathy is nothing more than the dynamic, social manifestation of *prajñā*, insight in action. If we are all one being, the one body of Vairocana, surely I can never consider my fate apart from the rest of the body; it must be all, or nothing. When I finally approach the point of ultimate perfection, which Hua-yen calls "entering the *dharma-dhātu*," then every being, to the last blade of grass, must enter the door together.

But where does my obligation end? It will be abundantly clear from preceding chapters that the interrelationships described by Hua-yen are not simply those among human beings, or even simply among living things. Whether the individual is a human being, a birch tree, or a stone, that individual exists *only* in dependence on all other things. But the human being is faced with a problem not shared by a stone; he must adopt an ethical stance toward all things, including water, soil, stone, and even human artifacts, which is consonant with this interdependence. First, whenever it is in my power, I must promote their destinies in the same way in which they indubitably promote mine. Second, looked at from the negative side, I must abstain from actions which interfere in their destinies, which detract from their integrity, and which degrade or nullify them. But I depend on these things in a number of ways, one of which is to use them for my own benefit. For I could not exist for a day if I did not use them. Therefore, in a world in which I must destroy and consume in order to continue to exist, I must use what is necessary with gratitude and respect. Part of this is a frugality born of this respect and gratitude, for to waste, out of greed or carelessness, is the rankest sort of ingratitude. It nullifies the thing we depend on, murders it, and in so doing, we murder ourselves and others. This attitude of respect and gratitude toward all things, which I would consider part of ethics, is extremely important in Buddhism, because it is not so much what one does, such as eating a carrot, as it is what one's attitude is toward that thing. No one ever became a Buddha, or entered the kingdom of heaven, who went through life with a careless, arrogant, hard-hearted attitude. Perhaps respect and gratitude are more important than we may think, ranking near the top of those modes of action we call ethics.

But there is one more point which will perhaps round out this discussion of attitudes and actions. That is the attitude of fair-mindedness. I must be prepared to accept the fact that I am made for the use of the other no less than it is made for my use. If I can really grasp this, then even though I may recoil and scream as the eager tiger pounces on me, which is natural for me to do, perhaps in the last moment of consciousness before I am gratefully consumed by the tiger, I may have the grace to reflect that this is the tiger's world as well as mine, and that I am for the use of hungry tigers just as much as carrots are for my use. Thus the least we can do is to be fair in our estimations as to the propriety of things.

These attitudes of respect, gratitude, fairness, and compassion, along with their embodiment in concrete acts, are reflected in several places in Hua-yen literature, and if nothing else, they are implied in the Hua-yen world picture. Compassion, mainly, is a common, even dominant theme in all Mahayana Buddhist literature, and in its recognition of the centrality of this attitude, Hua-yen takes its place in the development of Mahayana. We can find this emphasis on compassion in several places in Hua-yen literature. In the sutra literature, for instance, the primacy of compassion in Buddhas and Bodhisattvas is dealt with at length. In the chapter of the *Avataṁsaka Sūtra* named "The Arising of the *Tathāgata* from Essential Nature," for instance,[16] we can read a very elaborate discussion of how the Buddha appears in the world of time and space due to ten conditions. These conditions are, in essence, the needs of suffering beings, and thus this section of the sutra underlines an important fact of Buddhism, which is that Buddhas become Buddhas not out of any greed for self-spiritualization, but because as Buddhas they will have the proper equipment for carrying out their real mission, which is to help other beings. In the discussion of the three natures, it is clear that the absolute—the perfected nature—appears in the phenomenal world due to the condition of ignorance. That condition is, of course, the *avidyā* of those who are not Buddhas. It is because beings are in darkness and need light that a Buddha, out of a boundless compassion, appears to bring light. Indeed, if this were not a world of darkness, there would never be any need for them to appear bringing light, showing the Way.

But the Light of the World did appear, and he delivered a message which is, in essence, very simple: meditate and be compassionate, and the result will be serenity and peace, joy, light, and supreme service to ailing beings. It is the meditation which is the key, however, for the compassion does not come from an act of will, but is rather the outflow of meditation. This "meditation" (the term is unsatisfactory, but it has the virtue of familiarity) is traditionally divided into two parts, each part contributing to the overall goal. One part is *śamatha*, which traditionally had the office of tranquilizing those psychic factors which create obstacles to further progress (such as sense-desire and ill will). It has the general function of tranquilizing the self-perpetuating inner flow of hallucinations, daydreams, concepts, symbols, and judgment. According to Fa-tsang, *śamatha* consists of the increasing ability to see things as empty (*śūnya*).[17] The other part of the process is *vipaśyanā*, defined in older texts such as the *Visuddhimagga* as insight into the rising and falling of *dharmas* and their possession of the marks (*lakṣaṇa*) of impermanence, turmoil (*duḥkha*), nonself, and impurity (*aśubha*). Fa-tsang interprets *śamatha* and *vipaśyanā* respectively as leading to the insight into the emptiness of *dharmas* and leading to the knowledge that emptiness takes the form of *dharmas*; that is, there is no emptiness apart from form.[18] In his "Brief Commentary on the *Heart Sūtra*," Fa-tsang correlates *śamatha* with the sutra assertion that form is empty (*rūpam śūnyatā*) and *vipaśyanā* with the statement that emptiness itself is form (*śūnyataiva rūpam*). The importance of this dual form of meditation is that while the tranquility exercises produce the insight into emptiness, the analytic process leads to the very important perception of the fact that *there is something* of which it can be said that it is empty. Thus the Bodhisattva dwells in a world of other beings, and since this world of beings is one of identity and interdependence, there are obvious implications for activity.

When one practices tranquility and insight together, they are perfect. . . .

When one sees that form is empty, one achieves great wisdom and no longer dwells in *saṁsāra*. When one sees that emptiness is form, one achieves great compassion and does not dwell in *nirvāṇa*.[19]

Thus the Bodhisattva is "without an abiding place," free from attachment to both the mundane and the supramundane.

Meditation, as well as philosophy, is never an end in itself, but rather effects that transformation in the Bodhisattva which in turn transforms his perception of reality, and in so doing equips him for his true mission of emancipating all beings. But this mission is inextricably bound up with this perception; only in the Hua-yen *dharma-dhātu* as experienced by the individual are the vows of Samantabhadra possible. In the ordinary world as experienced by ordinary people, only competition and aggression, with their satellite impulses of fear, hatred, and suspicion, are possible.

Compassion, which I am considering to be an ethical matter here, is inextricably bound up with perception. As I remarked earlier, it is really only the dynamic form of *prajñā*-insight, which is itself the insight into emptiness. Why compassion develops along with insight will be readily apparent, if it is remembered that in Buddhism, to be compassionate really means to treat the other in conformity with what that object is in reality, divorced from illusion, wishfulness, inference, hearsay, convention, and the like. Simply stated, to act compassionately means to act in accordance with reality. As long as I always react to experience in terms of what is beneficial or harmful to my self, I can never really be of any effective use to others. When I am empty of a self, and when I no longer act in terms of selves, or within *any* conceptual framework, my relationship with the other will be that which the bystander would call "compassionate." Thus, as the *Vajracchedikā Sūtra* tells us, the Bodhisattva strives ceaselessly, leading all beings to the joy of *nirvāṇa*, but there never arises in him the concept of a being. In fact, it is only because no such thoughts arise that he does indeed lead all beings to *nirvāṇa*. Such a compassion is obviously not of the common variety, which is flawed with sentimentality, strained through erroneous concepts, and probably infected with some degree of ego need. We may, perhaps, think of it as "metaphysical compassion," to use Ananda Coomaraswamy's term.[20] We might even go so far as to call it love, but certainly no love that we know. Not the love of the mother for her child, not the love of Tristan for Isolde, and certainly not the love of a Marquis de Sade for his ladies; it is not like the love of the patriot for his country, or even like the love the worshiper feels for his god. Our experience of love is limited and self-interested. If anything, Buddhist love is something akin to that love of which Dante spoke so movingly and beautifully, as "the Love that moves the sun and the other stars." At first glance this may seem to be an outrageous exaggeration, but this compassion is not the compassion of the common man; it is the occurrence in space and time of a compassion which pervades ten thousand galaxies and realizes itself in them, individual by individual.

Someone once made the observation that one's skin is not necessarily a boundary marking off the self from the not-self but rather that which brings one into contact with the other. Like Faraday's electric charge which must be conceived as being everywhere, I am in some sense boundless, my being encompassing the farthest limits of the universe, touching and moving every atom in existence. The same is true of everything else. The interfusion, the sharing of destiny, is as infinite in scope as the reflections in the jewels of Indra's net. When in a rare moment I manage painfully to rise above a petty individualism by knowing my true nature, I perceive that I dwell in the wondrous net of Indra, and in this incredible network of interdependence, the career of the Bodhisattva must begin. It is not just that "we are all in it" together. We all *are* it, rising or falling as one living body.

Notes

(T. = *Taishō shinshū daizōkyō*. The following number is the number of the text in the *Taishō* collection, followed in turn by the page number and register.)

Chapter 1

1. Don Marquis, *The Lives and Times of Archy and Mahitabel* (New York: Doubleday, 1950), p. 56.
2. Mendel Sachs, "Space, Time and Elementary Interaction in Relativity," *Physics Today* (February 1969): 59. "The derived mass field depends upon the curvature of space-time. The latter geometrical property is, in turn, a manifestation of the mutual coupling of all the matter within the closed system. Thus, if the rest of the universe should be depleted of all matter, the mass of the remaining electron, say, should correspondingly go to zero. The derived field relationship is then a quantitative expression of the Mach principle because here the inertial mass of any amount of matter is indeed a well defined function of its dynamic coupling with all of the other matter within the entire closed system."
3. Daisetz T. Suzuki, *Zen and Japanese Culture*, Bolligen Series, vol. 64 (Princeton: Princeton University Press, 1971), p. 237.
4. T. 1866, p. 508c.
5. Thomas Berger, *Little Big Man* (New York: Dial Press, 1964), pp. 213–14.
6. Alfred North Whitehead, *The Concept of Nature* (Cambridge: Cambridge University Press, 1971), p. 146.
7. Sōgaku Harada Roshi, "On Practice," *Journal of the Zen Center of Los Angeles* (Winter 1973): 7.

Chapter 2

1. Such is the opinion of Japanese scholars involved in the Hua-yen tradition. The

most thorough study is Ishii Kyōdō, *Kegon kyōgaku seiritsu shi* (Tokyo: Chūō Koron Jigyō Shuppan, 1964). Other useful studies of the development of the sutra include Takamine Ryōshū, *Kegon shisō shi* (Kyoto: Kōkyō Shoin, 1942), and Kamekawa Kyōshin, *Kegongaku* (Kyoto: Hyakkaen, 1949). There is little question that the *Avataṁsaka* is the result of compilation of already existing sutras and new chapters composed specifically for the purpose of filling in gaps in structure. The *Daśabhūmika* and *Gaṇḍavyūha* existed both prior to and subsequent to the final compilation in the form of independent sutras. According to Kamekawa, the text has a close association with the Khotan region.

2. Other than the *Daśabhūmika* and *Gaṇḍavyūha*, the only other reference in Indian literature to the material now included in the *Avataṁsaka* consists of some verses from the chapter of the *A.* now called *Hsien shou*, in the *Śikṣāsamuccaya*. No other part of the *A.* seems to be mentioned elsewhere, which is surprising, if this text was known in Indian proper, since there is so much rich material on the Bodhisattva practices.

3. See the sources in note 1 above, for some of the evidence for this position.

4. Johannes Rahder, ed., *Daśabhūmika Sūtra* (Paris: Geuthner, 1926). The text has also been edited by Kondō Ryuko, *Daśabhūmīśvaro Nama Māhāyana Stotram* (Tokyo: Daigyō Bukkyō Kenkyōkai, 1936).

5. Daisetz T. Suzuki and Hokei Idzumi, eds., *The Gaṇḍavyūha Sūtra*, new rev. ed. (Tokyo: Sekai Seiten Kanko Kyōkai, 1959).

6. Kamata Shigeo, "Kegon-gaku no tenseki oyobi kenkyū bunken," in Kawada Kumatarō and Nakamura Hajime, eds., *Kegon shisō* (Tokyo: Hōzōkan, 1960), p. 517. Kamata concludes that most scholars now agree that Tu-shun should be considered the first patriarch.

7. Quoted in Heinrich Dumoulin, *History of Zen Buddhism* (New York: Pantheon, 1963), p. 38. Zen is "the practical consummation of Buddhist thought in China, and the Kegon (*Avataṁsaka*) philosophy is its theoretical culmination." "The philosophy of Zen is Kegon and the teaching of Kegon bears its fruit in the life of Zen."

8. Jan Fontein, *The Pilgrimage of Sudhana* (Netherlands: Mouton, 1967). The subtitle of Fontein's book is *A Study of Gaṇḍavyūha Illustrations in China, Japan, and Java*. It is the fullest and most thorough study to date of the vast amount of art in Asia centering around the episodes of the *Gaṇḍavyūha* section of the *Avataṁsaka*.

9. "Selections from the Chuang-tzu," in *Sources of Chinese Tradition*, ed. Theodore de Bary (New York: Columbia University Press, 1964), vol. 1. I have taken the liberty to alter the translation slightly, mostly in the use of some alternate translation equivalents. For the most part, I have adopted the suggestion of A.C. Graham, in his paper "Chuang-tzu's Essay on Seeing Things as Equal," in *History of Religions*, 9 (November and February 1969–70): 137–59, with regard to *shih* and *fei*. I have therefore translated these as "is" and "is not" respectively, instead of the more common "right" and "wrong."

10. Fung Yu-lan, *A Short History of Chinese Philosophy*, ed. Derk Bodde (New York: Macmillan Paperbacks, 1960), p. 221. I have altered this passage slightly, as in the previous quote, though the translation as such is that of Fung.

11. Ibid., p. 222.

12. The opening lines of the *Hsin hsin ming*, "The great Tao is not difficult, it simply does not choose," states the matter succinctly, and this is a well-known Buddhist poem. The point is not that we must avoid certain situations which may defile us or cause turmoil, but rather that the wise man is he who can mix with a world of light and shadow, pleasure and pain, life and death, and not be thrown off balance by them. The persistent Taoist attitude is that of neither exulting in victory nor despairing in defeat. Kuo-hsiang says, in his commentary on the *Chuang-tzu*, "If one is contented wherever he goes, he will be at ease wherever he goes. Even life and death can not affect him. How much less can flood and fire? The perfect man is not besieged by calamities, not because he escapes from them but because he advances the principles of things." [Wing-Tsit Chan, trans., *A Source Book in Chinese Philosophy* (Princeton: Princeton University Press Paperback, 1969), p. 328.] Both the Indian and Chinese approaches to the higher life can be considered to be simply alternate methods of achieving equilibrium in one's responses to experience. The Chinese approach was not to eliminate certain personality factors or avoid certain experiences, but to confront any circumstance without permitting it to cause attachment or loathing. It was a question of flexibility.

13. My argument here is simply that there were important areas of agreement between Taoist and Buddhist ideas. This is not to deny that there were areas of Buddhist thought which had no Taoist equivalent, nor would I deny that the use of Taoist terms as substitutes for the Sanskrit sometimes gave shades of meaning to the Indian concept which were foreign to it. This is particularly true of the early period, in about the third and fourth centuries. I am only saying that one of the reasons why Chinese with a scholarly or literary leaning became attracted to Buddhism is that they saw in Buddhism certain concepts, and certain ways of handling experience, which seemed familiar to them. One particular instance of this agreement lay in the teaching of the Śūnyavāda sutras that emancipation consisted in a nonconceptual mode of experience, wherein the normal symbolic, conceptual, categorizing function of the mind ceased to serve as a mediating link between the bare datum and its awareness in the subject. In other words, the world was to be known in its suchness, *tathatā*, rather than in its conceptual, conventional form. A Chinese gentleman versed in the writings of Lao-tzu and Chuang-tzu was bound to find this a familiar concept, though ultimately his way of thinking about the matter owed more to the Taoist classics than to Indian modes of thought. As I have indicated in the quotations in the text, the Indian picture of existence as interdependent tallied very well with the convictions of Chuang-tzu and Neo-taoists such as Kuo-hsiang.

14. Apparently the kind of identity which so greatly interested men such as Fa-tsang was first explored systematically and seriously during the period of the division between North and South China and during the succeeding Sui period by such monks as Seng-tsan and Hui-yüan (i.e., not the contemporary of Kumārajīva but a later Hui-yüan). In his *Ta-ch'eng i chang* Hui-yüan devotes a lot of space to the discussion of *dharmas* as being alike in essence and different in function, a style of treatment which later became standard for the Hua-yen thinkers. For a full discussion of this, see Kamata Shigeo, *Chūgoku bukkyō shisō shi kenkyū* (Tokyo: Shunjūsha, 1968), pp. 313–14, 349–50. Kamata sees this activity as being in part an attempt on the part of the sangha to reconcile the secular and sacred orders, and this need to equate Buddhism with the secular order must in turn

be seen against the background of Northern Chinese Buddhism of the period, which had to function in a totalitarian state (pp. 272–74). He sees the rock carvings of Buddhas with the faces of the Emperor, at Yun-kang and Lung-men, as a further indication of the attempt by the sangha to say that there is no difference between the Buddha and the Emperor (p. 279).

15. I tend to see Tu-shun and Chih-yen as continuing the work of the Ti-lun and She-lun scholars in supplying the pieces that were finally to be assembled by Fa-tsang. This is not to disparage the real contributions of Chih-yen, whose writings show an important attempt at being systematic and thorough, but his work is simple and incomplete compared to that of Fa-tsang. The Hua-yen system as a coherent whole emerges for the first time in the essays of Fa-tsang. The last two masters, Ch'eng-kuan and Tsung-mi, refined, defined, filled in details, and gave the Hua-yen system particular orientations dictated by their own special interests, *wei-shih* epistemology and Ch'an meditation respectively. Fa-tsang was not especially noteworthy as an original thinker, but he was a powerful thinker, and obviously had an exceptional talent for organizing and syncretizing a large body of fragments. Without his talent for seeing the interrelationships of these parts, and without the learning needed to give ideas a traditional support, it is safe to say that there would not have been a Hua-yen tradition.

16. As the title indicates, the essay is primarily concerned with *śamatha-vipaśyanā* exercises (*shih-kuan*), which is to say, with meditation. It is thought that the extant essay is not by Tu-shun, but was composed by Fa-tsang, who utilized material originating with Tu-shun. See, for instance, Kamata, "Kegon-gaku no tenseki oyobi kenkyū bunken," in *Kegon Shisō*, p. 504. Other fragments of Tu-shun's work are found in Chih-yen's *Hua-yen i-ch'eng shih hsüan men* (T. 1868).

17. See the above note for Tu-shun's contributions. Chih-yen's comments on meditation are interspersed throughout his writings, particularly in the lengthy *Sou hsüan chi* (T. 1732). Fa-tsang wrote a treatise named *Hua-yen ta p'u-t'i hsin chang*, which is also named *Hua-yen san-mei chang* (T. 1878). His *Pan-lo-po-mi-to hsin ching lio shu*, which is a running commentary on the *Prajñāpāramitā Hridaya Sūtra*, contains interesting comments on the relation of the message of the sutra to *śamatha* and *vipaśyanā*. Ch'eng-kuan also dealt with practice, continuing the Hua-yen concern with *san-mei* (*samādhi*) and meditation in general. His *San cheng yüan-yung kuan men* (T. 1882), particularly, is concerned with meditation. Tsung-mi was probably most concerned of all Hua-yen masters with meditation, which is not surprising, because he was also a Ch'an master. He wrote much on meditation and general Bodhisattva practices in most of his work, but *Chu Hua-yen fa-chiai kuan men* (T. 1884) is one of the most important works concerned with this matter. He taught throughout his writings that there is no real separation between meditation and study.

Chapter 3

1. Almost all of Buddhist thought may be seen as one prolonged concern with the problem of causation. Such central Buddhist doctrines as *śūnyatā*, *pratītyasamutpāda*, and *apohavāda*, as well as a great amount of the psychological work of the Theravādins, the *dharma* theory of the Sarvāstivādins, and the complicated structure of the eight *vijñānas* of the Vijñānavādins, may all be seen, for instance, as basically concerned with the problem of causation. Hua-yen, inasmuch as the core of its system is concerned with a species of *pratītyasamutpāda*, is a continuation of this ancient problem. Richard Robinson has said that "causation [was] a central problem throughout the history of Indian philosophy" in *The Buddhist Religion. A Historical Introduction* (Belmont, Calif.: Dickenson, 1970), p. 21. He also makes the point, in *Early Mādhyamika in India and China* (Madison: University of Wisconsin Press, 1967), that causation was the central Indian Buddhist problematic (p. 161).

2. Quoted by D.S. Ruegg, in *La théorie du tathāgatagarbha et du gotra* (Paris: Ecole Française d'Extreme-Orient, 1969), p. 299. The text quoted is the *Anūnatvāpurṇatvanirdeśaparivarta*, which is also cited several times in Fa-tsang's Treatise. There is a rather long list of synonyms which Buddhism uses freely when referring to the absolute. Ruegg also mentions the *Avataṁsaka* itself (p. 286 ff.) as assimilating *tathāgatagarbha* to Buddha *jñāna* and *Tathāgata jñāna*. According to him (p. 265) the text mentioned above also equates *tathāgatagarbha* with *dharma-kāya*.

3. The monograph of D.S. Ruegg, mentioned in the preceding note, is the only full-length work in a Western language devoted exclusively to the doctrine of *tathāgatagarbha*.

4. T.R.V. Murti, *The Central Philosophy of Buddhism* (London: Allen and Unwin, 1955); Frederick Streng, *Emptiness: A Study in Religious Meaning* (Nashville: Abingdon, 1967); Robinson, *Early Mādhyamika in India and China*. Edward Conze has written much about the doctrine of emptiness, and his translations of the literature are well known. Among his many books might be mentioned *Buddhist Thought in India* (Ann Arbor: University of Michigan Press, 1967) and *Buddhist Wisdom Books* (London: Hillary, 1958).

5. Mentioned by Conze in *Buddhist Thought in India*, p. 195. He mentions Regamey, Schayer, and Falk as some of those who hold this theory.

6. I am paraphrasing Dr. Conze, which will make him unhappy, I fear. In *Selected Sayings from the Perfection of Wisdom* (London: Buddhist Society, 1955), p. 18, he says of the vast literature on the perfection of wisdom, "What then is the *subject matter*? It is just the Unconditioned, nothing but the Absolute over and over again."

7. Jacques May, *Candrakīrti Prasannapadā Madhyamakavṛtti* (Paris: Adrien-Maisonneuve, 1959), p. 222. My translation from the French.

8. Ibid.

9. Ibid., p. 223.

10. Ruegg, in *La théorie du tathāgatagarbha et du gotra*, p. 362 ff., devotes several pages to the problem. He finds the *Ratnagotravibhāga* (*Uttaratantra*) to be one of the main sources of this tendency, in its habit of describing the *dharma-kāya* or *tathāgatagarbha* through the use of positive epithets—i.e., tranquil, permanent, stabile. According to Ruegg (p. 319 ff.), there was a tendency in Tibet, exemplified by the Jo naṅ pa sect, to find in the doctrine of the "emptiness of the other" (*gźan stoṅ*) a basis for the positive description of emptiness/

tathāgatagarbha. There is, of course, a very old tradition in Buddhism, observable in Pali literature, of referring to *nirvāṇa* as "a refuge," "cool," "a ford," etc. In Mahayana literature, there is a tendency to speak of *nirvāṇa* in terms diametrically opposed to those which refer to *saṁsāra*—permanent, possessing self, blissful, and extremely pure. However, such terms are usually interpreted as mere verbal devices used to lure the individual away from his attachment to ordinary existence. Occasionally, however, there has been a tendency to think of such terms as really describing the indescribable. The same may be said of the custom in Far Eastern Buddhism of speaking of a "Great Self" which is realized upon the destruction of the fictional concept of the mundane *ātman*. Ruegg (p. 371) says that the *Mahāyānasūtra-ālamkāra* also speaks of a *mahā-ātman* and defends its use as a convenient concept.

11. Robinson, *Early Mādhyamika*, p. 43.

12. Ibid., p. 49.

13. May, *Candrakīrti Prasannapadā Madhyamakavṛtti*, p. 224.

14. Murti, *Central Philosophy*, pp. 212–13.

15. Non-Buddhist opponents of the Śūnyavādins often accused them of nihilism, as can be seen in Nāgārjuna's *Mādhyamika-kārikās*, where he takes pains to refute the charge. I tend to interpret Hua-yen as a Chinese restatement of the Śūnyavāda position, in which the predominant negative approach of Nāgārjuna's school has been eliminated. One indication of the Chinese desire to give a positive connotation to emptiness may possibly be found in a strong tendency in Chinese Buddhist treatises to substitute the old, tradition-laden term *li* for "emptiness." *Li*, as the principle by which things are themselves, or as the pattern of order that runs through nature, is similar in tone to emptiness interpreted as interdependent being, but whereas "emptiness" has, at least in its semantic force, the connotations of voidness, nullity, and the like, *li* connotes only the full, rich, creative potential that lies at the root of the phenomenal world. Fa-tsang substitutes *li* frequently for "emptiness," and in fact he uses both terms interchangeably throughout his writings. Thus in his mind, both terms meant the same, but *li* had a positive ring seemingly lacking in *śūnyatā*.

16. Alfred North Whitehead, *Science and the Modern World* (New York: Macmillan, 1926), p. 275.

17. Ruegg, *La théorie du tathāgatagarbha*, p. 516.

18. Ibid., pp. 78, 126, 267. "In other words, while the *tathāgatagarbha* is so to speak assimilable to the *dharma-kāya* of the *tathāgata*, the *tathāgatagarbha* of living beings who are affected by the *kleśa* and still bound to the cycle of existences is not simply identical to the *dharma-kāya* of the perfect Buddha on the plane of Result" (p. 267; my translation). The temptation to make a simple, unqualified identification results from the idea that the *tathāgatagarbha* or *dharma-kāya* is utterly nondual. Since it is nondual, if it is the true basis for all living things, then all must be perfect Buddhas. However, it is only the embryo or seed of Buddhahood, in need of nurturing, and the living being is obviously not endowed with such marks of full Buddhahood as the thirty-two marks or the eighteen special qualities. The *tathāgatagarbha* is thus something similar to musical talent; it exists

both in the beginning violinist and in Heifitz, but in one it needs training to become the glorious miracle it is in the other.

19. Ibid., pp. 109, 117, 189, 405.

20. Ibid., pp. 315, 403. The *Ratnagotravibhāga* also mentions the same identification, quoting the *Śrīmālādevī Sūtra*.

21. As Richard Robinson points out, in *Early Mādhyamika in India and China* (pp. 96–114), some members of the early Chinese sangha such as Hui-yüan never did really understand the doctrine of emptiness, particularly in the form it has in Mādhyamika treatises. However, Fa-tsang had the benefit of almost three more centuries of work on the part of his predecessors, and by his time, members of the sangha seem for the most part to have correctly assimilated the concept. Some of the evidence of Fa-tsang's grasp of the doctrine can be seen in Chapter 7 of this book. See also my translation of, and commentary on, Fa-tsang's "Brief Commentary on the *Heart Sūtra*," in *Buddhist Meditation: Theory and Practice* (Honolulu: University Press of Hawaii, 1976).

22. Treatise, T. 1866, p. 502c.

23. *Bukkyō taikei: go kyō shō* (Tokyo: Bukkyō Taikei Kanseikai, 1923), 2:46–47. Gyōnen's point is that both the "six meanings" and Nāgārjuna's "eight negations" are simply alternate approaches to the same problem. "This shows that in the Dharma there is [the teaching method of] obstructing and manifesting, of doing away with common-sense [conceptions] or revealing the true principle" (p. 46). "Obstructing and manifesting, or opposing [the false] and revealing [the true] are simply two sides of the same coin" (p. 46). As Fa-tsang's statement shows, both approaches deal with *pratītyasamutpāda*, but the connotations of the eight negations are negative, while those of the six meanings are positive.

24. See Chapter 2, n. 13.

25. *T'an hsüan chi*, T. vol. 35, p. 346c. Fa-tsang says that Vairocana pervades both kinds of *karma*-result, as innate *prajñā* and as the material world-receptacle. Thus the full Buddha-*prajñā* is present in things, not just as a seed-potential. The *Avataṁsaka*, in the chapter "The Appearance of the *Tathāgata*," says that *prajñā* is present in the bodies of all sentient beings. In principle, it is present in everything, including nonsentient things.

26. This Hui-yüan lived during the North and South dynasties and Sui dynasty. He was very much interested in this whole line of questioning. His commentary on the *Ch'i hsin lun* discusses the idea that *tathatā* is a mixture of the pure and impure, and in his *Ta-ch'eng i chang*, he discusses how *dharmas* are both the same and different. Fa-tsang either knew Hui-yüan's work or else can be seen as perpetuating the sort of speculation that occurred in the several generations preceding his own time. He frequently uses the same terminology that Hui-yüan uses, or, as is often the case in his Treatise, he uses alternate expressions such as "immutability" and "conditionedness," while the patterns of thought themselves are usually identical with those of Hui-yüan. Sometimes he uses both sets of terms in the same passage: "Obeying conditions and arising and ceasing is the category of arising and ceasing. That is to say, in compliance with influences it [i.e., *tathatā*] becomes active and forms impure and pure [*dharmas*]. Even though impure and pure form its nature, it is eternally unmoving. Moreover, it is able to become the impure and pure because it does not become active. Therefore, it can be said to be active without being disturbed" (T. vol. 44, p. 251b, c).

27. T. vol. 44, no. 1846.

28. *Bukkyō taikei*, 2:29–30. "The interpenetrating *dharma-dhātu* is the body of the Buddha, and is called *Dharma-dhātu* Buddha."

29. Quoted in Saitō Yuishin, *Kegon-gaku kōyō* (Tokyo: Shūseisha, 1920), pp. 158–59. Fa-tsang's thought bears a strong resemblance to that of such earlier thinkers as Hui-chao, who, in his commentary on the *Suvarṇaprabhāsottama Sūtra*, gives four meanings of the word "mind": mind as *tathatā*; mind as that which thinks; mind as the accumulation of experience; and mind as *ālaya-vijñāna*. Fa-tsang means mind as *tathatā* when he speaks of the universe as mind only. This latter information is derived from Kametani Shōkei, *Kegon tetsugaku kenkyū* (Tokyo: Meikyō Gakkai, 1922), p. 94. I have not seen Hui-chao's commentary.

30. Each thing is the *garbha* or womb of Buddhahood inasmuch as it embraces or conceals (*ts'ang*) intrinsically pure *tathatā*. According to Kamata Shigeo, in *Chūgoku bukkyō shisō shi no kenkyū* (Tokyo: Zaidan Hōjin Tokyo Daigaku, 1965), pp. 13–15, although the *Mahāparinirvāṇa Sūtra* says that only living beings really possess Buddha nature, the Chinese, under the influence of Taoist thought, tended to say that all things have it, just as all things have Tao nature.

31. Treatise, T. 1866, p. 499b.

32. Ibid., p. 499a.

33. Ibid., p. 501c.

Chapter 4

1. According to Hsüan-tsang's *Ch'eng wei-shih lun*, "*Pariniṣpanna* is eternal freedom of *paratantra* from the *parikalpita* nature." Since his discussion of the three natures is made purely from the standpoint of consciousness as the sole reality, he also says that "the name *Pariniṣpanna* is also given to the 'pure conditioned,' that is to say, the pure mind which is *Paratantra*" [Wei Tat, trans., *Ch'eng wei-shih lun* (Hong Kong: Ch'eng Wei Shih Lun, 1973), p. 635]. The *Mahāyānasaṃgraha* says of *pariniṣpanna*, "It is the complete absence of all objective character [i.e., imputed character] in the dependent nature" [My translation of the French of Etienne Lamotte, trans., *La Somme du Grand Véhicule* (Louvain: Bibliotheque du Muséon, 1938), 2:91. I have altered Wei Tat's translation slightly].

2. Kamata Shigeo, *Chūgoku kegon shisō shi no kenkyū* (Tokyo: Zaidan Hōjin Tokyo Daigaku, 1965), pp. 144–48. Fa-tsang and the Empress Wu had a need for each other, apparently. Fa-tsang needed the imperial patronage, and the Empress was interested in the ability of Hua-yen thought to furnish a rationale for her relationship to her subjects and for the relationship of imperial T'ang China to satellite countries. Also, having usurped the throne from her predecessor, who had patronized Hsüan-tsang's Wei-shih school, the new patronage of Hua-yen and the withdrawal of patronage from Hsüan-tsang's school had an obvious symbolic value.

3. Treatise, T. 1866, p. 499a.

4. Ibid.

5. Nagao Gadjin, "Some problems in Fa-tsang's discussion of the three natures," in *Fifty-Year Anniversary Commemorative Anthology of the Kyoto University Department of Arts and Letters* (Kyoto, 1957), p. 186. (In Japanese)

6. Louis de La Vallée Poussin, trans., "Le petit traité de Vasubandhu-Nāgārjuna sur les trois natures," *Mélanges Chinois et Bouddhiques* 2-3 (1932–35): 158.

7. Ibid., pp. 158–59.

Nispanna does not differ from *kalpita*, because the second has for its nature the duality which does not exist, because the first has for its nature the inexistence of this duality.

Kalpita does not differ from *nispanna*, because the second has for its nature the inexistence of duality, because the first has for its nature nonduality.

Nispanna does not differ from *paratantra*, because the second does not exist as it appears, because the first has for its nature the inexistence of this mode of appearance.

Paratantra does not differ from *nispanna*, because the second is the self-nature of the duality which does not exist, because the first does not have for its nature its mode of appearance. [My translation from the French]

8. Treatise, T. 1866, p. 503b. Fa-tsang is not, of course, falling into some terrible non-Buddhist error of asserting a *svabhāva*, let alone two of them. "Different essence" and "identical essence" are not *svabhāvas* of the sort denied by Buddhism. This will be clear if it is remembered that "identical essence" is nothing more than the identity shared by all *dharmas* in their complete lack of a *svabhāva*; that is, their common or identical essence is essencelessness. "Different essence" is simply a reference to the obvious fact of the difference in form and function among *dharmas*.

9. The following quotation in the text gives his reason for this statement. His argument in his analogy of the building (Ch. 6) is that if the rafter is not integrated into the building, the total building will not come into being. To be complete, the building depends on the rafter.

10. *Bukkyō taikei*, 1:65.

11. Treatise, T. 1866, p. 503b, c.

Chapter 5

1. *Bukkyō taikei* (Tokyo: Bukkyō Taikei Kanseikai, 1923), 2:65.

2. Ibid. p. 54.

3. Yusugi Ryōei, *Kegon-gaku gairon* (Kyoto: Ryūtani University Publishing Bureau, 1941), p. 127.

4. I am not thinking of any particular passage in Whitehead's writings. Rather, the

whole of *Process and Reality* and much in a book such as *Modes of Thought* involve the idea that anything which we may call a reality, an existent, is the product of antecedent causes and is itself one cause for a subsequent reality. All of existence is thus bound up with causation, so that to exist means to be caused and to be a cause. Whatever is removed from causation is a nonentity. For Whitehead, reality is process, and process is the never-ending transformation of the universe into ever-new realities, in a perpetual cause-effect flow. However, for Hua-yen and Whitehead alike, in the final analysis, the causal entity should not really be considered to be very substantial, and certainly not permanent, for what is conventionally considered to be a cause is itself only the momentary result of antecedent causes and perishes so soon that to think of it as a *real* point analyzable from process itself is to invest it with a false permanence. Whitehead agrees with Hua-yen that the "what" of an entity can really only be understood when seen as the "how" of the thing; i.e., as the sum total of contributory causes and as a causal link in a ceaseless process.

5. The "universal eye" or "universal vision" is one of several types of "eye" enumerated in Buddhist literature. Here it contrasts with the corporeal eye, which can only see material objects, and then usually incorrectly. The universal eye is an intuitive vision within *samādhi* which sees the real nature of things as identical and interdependent, which is undetectable by the corporeal eye. It was Chih-yen, the second patriarch of Hua-yen, who first claimed that the perfection of the Hua-yen school rested on the fact that its teachings were the expression of the universal vision of the Buddha in the *sāgara-mudrā samādhi*.

6. Quoted in Saitō Yuishin, *Kegon-gaku kōyō* (Tokyo: Shūseisha, 1920), p. 60. I have not been able to trace his reference.

7. For the meaning of the name, see Mochizuki Shinkō, *Bukkyō daijiten*, 1:376–77. Other sources that discuss this *samādhi* are Kamata Shigeo, *Chūgoku bukkyō shisō shi kenkyū* (Tokyo: Zaidan Hōjin Daigaku, 1965), pp. 403–6, and Kamekawa Kyōshin, *Kegon-gaku* (Kyoto: Hyakkaen, 1949), pp. 17–19. All these scholars gloss *in* with the compound *in-hsien*, the latter part of the compound meaning "to manifest," "to appear," and the like, or *in-hsiang*, the latter word meaning "appearance" or "image." I believe it is clear that the translation of *in* as "seal" reveals an ignorance of the simile which gives the *samādhi* its name.

Chapter 6

1. Treatise, T. 1866, p. 507c ff.

2. This is Vasubandhu's commentary on the *Daśabhūmika Sūtra*, T. 1522, pp. 124c–125a.

3. The most useful commentaries are Gyōnen's *Tsūroki*, Shih-hui's *Wu chiao chang fu ku chi*, and the *Kegon go kyō shō shi ji ki*, all of which can be found in *Bukkyō taikei* (Tokyo: Bukkyō Taikei Kanseikai, 1923), vols. 13 and 14. At this point in the Treatise, all the commentaries become very brief and perfunctory, probably because the example is so clear and self-explanatory and because the details were explained in earlier sections of the commentaries.

4. T. 1881. This is a very short essay, and while it is not nearly so detailed and systematic as the Treatise, it is very useful for getting some idea of the inner workings of the Hua-yen system. Much of it has to do with the "six characteristics." Fa-tsang used a gold statue of a lion as a means of demonstrating to the Empress Wu the nature of identity and interpenetration. There is a translation into English in Wing-Tsit Chan, *Source Book in Chinese Philosophy* (Princeton: Princeton University Press, 1969), pp. 409–24.

5. While I am aware of the objections some of my colleagues in philosophy will have with regard to 'the linguistic and logical problems involved in this identification of "universal" and "particular," extensive research has convinced me that these are the proper translation terms for the Chinese and that Fa-tsang does indeed say that they are identical. I believe that a close reading of the Treatise will resolve their fears and doubts. "Whole" and "part" are also used as equivalents in the Treatise. In that text, on p. 507c, Fa-tsang uses the Chinese word *ping* as an equivalent, and Yusugi Ryōei, in his *Kegon-gaku gairon* (Kyoto: Ryutani University Publishing Bureau, 1941), p. 150, says that "it is the building which universalizes the pillars, rafters, and so on."

6. Yusugi Ryōei, in *Daizōkyō kōza: go kyō shō kōgi* (Tokyo: Tōhō Shoin, 1932), p. 39, speaks of four kinds of Samantabhadra: Samantabhadra as the Dharma; Samantabhadra as *prajñā*; Samantabhadra as practice; and Samantabhadra as all living beings. According to Yusugi, all who practice the Dharma are Samantabhadra. One does not distinguish between holy and profane, since in respect to the realm of Samantabhadra, one is either on the early, middle, or later stages of practice, but all are alike Samantabhadra.

7. These vows are dealt with extensively in the *Avataṁsaka*, which is nothing but a detailed description of the progress of the disciple from the earliest stage of training up through perfect enlightenment. Thus each vow is dealt with in detail. However, this enumeration of vows can be found in the translation of the *Samantabhadracarī-praṇidhāna*, by Prajñā. For a discussion of these vows, see Kaneko Daiei, *Kegon-gyō gaisetsu* (Kyoto: Zenjinsha, 1948), pp. 130 ff.

8. The names and arrangement of the six characteristics make this quite evident, but the variety of names may give the impression that something more than part and whole, or one and many, are being discussed. See Saitō Yuishin, *Kegon-gaku kōyō* (Tokyo: Shūseisha, 1920), p. 175, and Kamekawa Kyōshin, *Kegon-gaku* (Kyoto: Hyakkaen, 1949), pp. 256 ff.

Chapter 7

1. *Tōdai-ji*, published by Tōdai-ji, Nara, n.d.

2. Tu-shun, *Hua-yen wu chiao shih kuan*, T. 1867, p. 513c.

3. All of Hua-yen literature, particularly the writings of Fa-tsang, speak of Vairocana as the "Buddha with ten bodies." See his Treatise, for instance, T. 1866, pp. 498c, 499a.

4. Quoted by Dōgen, in *Seizei sanshoku*, in his *Shōbōgenzō*. *Zenyaku Shōbōgenzō*, ed. Nakamura Sōichi (Tokyo: Seishin Shobō, 1971), 1:438.

5. Quoted in Fa-tsang's Treatise, T. 1866, p. 500b.

6. *Ta-ch'eng fa-chiai wu ch'a-pieh lun shu*, T. 1838.

7. Treatise, T. 1866, p. 499a.

8. T. 1733, p. 214c.

9. For an excellent discussion of the creativity and potential of emptiness, see Hisamatsu Shinichi, "The Characteristics of Oriental Nothingness," *Philosophical Studies of Japan* 2 (1960): 65–97. Buddhists use several terms to denote the same thing—emptiness, Buddha, Buddha-nature, nonbeing, *tathāgatagarbha*, and *dharma-dhātu*, to name a few. A very interesting treatment of emptiness can also be found in Nishida Kitarō, *A Study of Good*, trans. V.H. Viglielmo (Tokyo: Printing Bureau of the Japanese Government, 1960).

10. Treatise, T. 1866, p. 501b, c.

11. *Pan-lo-po-lo-mi-to hsin ching lio shu*, T. 1712, p. 553a.

12. Ibid., p. 553c.

13. Richard Robinson, *Early Mādhyamika in India and China* (Madison: University of Wisconsin Press, 1967), p. 140. Seng-chao refutes the view that "emptiness is the primordial inexistence from which all existent things have arisen . . . so that inexistence is the matrix of everything."

14. *Pan-lo-po-lo-mi-to hsin ching lio shu*, T. 1712, p. 553a, b.

15. Both of the sources quoted by Fa-tsang make the point that if emptiness is inexistent, there can be no modification ever in the status quo. In other words, according to the understanding of *svabhāva* held by the Śūnyavādins, it is only because *dharmas* are empty, which is to say have no self-existence, that they are able to change in dependence upon conditions. I believe that Fa-tsang understood this point very well. The Hua-yen *dharma-dhātu* is if anything a constantly changing configuration as a whole and at every point in the structure. There is no thing anywhere that does not constantly change in this manner; indeed, given a perpetual, instantaneous change at all points, there cannot even be "things" as commonly understood.

16. *Pan-lo-po-lo-mi-to hsin ching lio shu*, T. 1712, p. 553c.

17. Ibid.

18. *Hua-yen wu chiao shih kuan*, T. 1867, p. 511a.

19. This should not be mistaken to mean that emptiness is another entity apart from concrete reality, nor should it be taken to mean that emptiness is *in* the world, as some sort of pantheistic immanence. On the other hand, this does not mean that the natural world as ordinarily perceived is the object of devotion and reverence, resulting in simple nature worship or a quasi-religious estheticism. It is the world in its identity and interdependence, which is to say its emptiness, which is revered as the body of the Buddha. If emptiness is the mode of being of things, then we can understand Fa-tsang's assertion that neither things nor emptiness can have an independent existence.

20. T. vol. 14, p. 542. This is quoted in the Treatise, p. 500b. The passage quoted can not be found in that identical form in the *Taishō* text. Fa-tsang has paraphrased material found there.

21. T. vol. 16, p. 467. Quoted in the Treatise, p. 499a. The quote cannot be found in this form in the text cited by Fa-tsang. He has paraphrased material from that source. The five "paths" are those of *devas*, humans, animals, *pretas*, and beings in the hells. Some texts have six paths, adding that of the *asuras*.

22. Buddhism does not deny the concrete world of things when it says that they do not exist. The denial is always of the world as we experience it, mediated by concepts which are superimposed upon it. Our world is always a mental world, not the real, vibrant world of *tathatā*. Enlightenment restores our contact with reality.

23. From the Chinese "new translation" of the *Avataṁsaka* by Śikṣānanda, during the early T'ang period. This verse is from the chapter called "Peak of Sumeru," T. 279. The "old translation" by Buddhabhadra (T. 278) has an equivalent verse in the chapter called "Yama Heavens":

> All *dharmas* are birthless
> And also are not extinguished.
> If one can understand this,
> He sees the *Tathāgata*.

24. This chapter was originally published in a different form in *Philosophy East and West* 22 (October 1972):403–15.

Chapter 8

1. Treatise, T. 1866, p. 491a, b. "The foolish worldling acquires rebirth when his *karma* is nourished by the active defilements. Holy persons are not the same. They acquire rebirth [in *saṁsāra*] only through the retention of the latent potentialities of the defilements." This whole section of the Treatise, entitled "The Body Which Supports Practices," and the following section, "Extinguishing Defilements," (p. 492b) deal extensively with this matter. The point is that the retention of some *kleśa* is an intentional act on the part of the Bodhisattva. See also ibid., p. 493a; "Even though [the Bodhisattva] has the ability to freely extinguish the obstacles of defilement from the first stage on, he deliberately retains them and does not extinguish them. Why? In order to nourish rebirth and attract and convert others."

2. Daisetz T. Suzuki, trans., *The Laṅkāvatāra Sūtra* (London: Routledge and Kegan Paul, 1932), p. 184. "Mahāmati, when the Bodhisattvas face and perceive the happiness of the Samādhi of perfect tranquilization, they are moved with the feeling of love and sympathy owing to their original vows, and they become aware of the part they are to perform as regards the [ten] inexhaustible vows. Thus they do not enter Nirvana. But the fact is that they are already in Nirvana, because in them there is no rising of discrimination."

3. H. Kern, trans., *Saddharma-puṇḍarīka or The Lotus of the True Law* (Oxford: Clarendon Press, 1884), p. 302. "And even now, young gentlemen of good family, I have not accomplished my ancient Bodhisattva-course, and the measure of my lifetime is not full." (This is vol. 21 of the *Sacred Books of the East*.)

4. From *Hotsu bodai shin*. Quoted in Okada Sembō, *Shōbōgenzō shisō taikei* (Tokyo: Hosei University Press, 1959), 6:17–18.

5. This is the Māhāyana idea of "self-benefit and benefit to others," or "self-benefit is benefiting others." It means that by acquiring enlightenment oneself, one may be able to help others. It may also be said that constant activity on behalf of others helps oneself to grow spiritually. It sounds a little like the Western principle of enlightened self-interest, but the Bodhisattva does not pursue his own good in some sort of "trickle-down" theory of social amelioration, nor does he help others with the attitude that like bread upon the waters, he will be repaid a hundredfold. The *true* Bodhisattva is utterly selfless. In his complete devotion to the welfare of all living beings, he does grow in insight and compassion. From the standpoint of *his* practices, his only reason for seeking enlightenment is that this is the only *real* way he can help others. Either way, his thoughts are always on helping others, which is the essence of the Bodhisattva.

6. Treatise, T. 1866, p. 489b.

7. Ibid., p. 489c–490a. Fa-tsang also says (484b), "The Bodhisattva exhausts the practices of the whole *dharma-dhātu* in all the worlds in the ten directions, yet he does not divide his body. He fills the worlds everywhere simultaneously and in a single instant cultivates all practices universally."

8. Ibid., p. 490a.

9. Ibid.

10. "Intrinsic enlightenment" is none other than Buddha-nature, or Buddha *jñāna*, which is an innate aspect of all living beings (and perhaps of nonliving beings). It is easily assimilated to the concept of *tathāgatagarbha*, the subject of Chapter 3. This intrinsic enlightenment, however, always exists as a mere potentiality up to the time the individual begins to "nourish" it by means of practice, meaning meditation for the most part. What is ordinarily considered to be enlightenment, the historical event, is the coalescing of intrinsic enlightenment and "acquired" enlightenment, which is just the culmination of practice. This historical event is called "initial enlightenment." The doctrine of sudden enlightenment is only indirectly concerned with the question of the length of time it takes to perfect training or the length of time of the enlightenment event. Rather, in such thinkers as Hui-neng and Dōgen, sudden enlightenment is claimed on the basis of the beginningless existence of intrinsic enlightenment in the individual. In Dōgen's Sōtō Zen, for instance, meditation is considered to be the means of manifesting, or *real*-izing, this intrinsic enlightenment, not a means of creating enlightenment. This is the Zen of sudden enlightenment because one is always enlightened right from the beginning, and practice is based on intrinsic enlightenment.

11. Dōgen seems to have inherited the sudden enlightenment teachings of Hui-neng. His essays in *Shōbōgenzō* are full of admonitions not to think of meditation as a means of becoming enlightened, and the reason for this, as was pointed out in the preceding note, is that one already is enlightened. Thus in *Fukan zazengi* he says, "The Way is essentially perfect and all-pervading. How can one thus seek the Way or realize it? The Truth which carries us along is sovereign and does not require our efforts. It completely excels anything

of this world. Who can believe in the expedient of purifying the mind [literally, "mirror-wiping"]? The truth is always right at hand" [Tamaki Koshirō, ed. and trans., *Dōgen shū*, 2:49, in *Nihon no shisō* (Tokyo: Chikuma Shobō, 1969)]. Dōgen also says (*Dōgen shū*, p. 53), "That which is called *zazen* is not a way of developing concentration. It is simply the way of comfort. It is a practice which measures your enlightenment to the fullest extent." See, also, his *Bendōwa*, which contains many passages of this nature.

12. Fa-tsang discusses the school of sudden enlightenment often throughout his Treatise, so it seems to have been a matter of common knowledge by the end of the seventh century. This was also the time of Hui-neng, a contemporary of Fa-tsang. As I have pointed out in the two preceding notes, the Chinese preference for what is called "sudden enlightenment" seems to have found its doctrinal basis in the concept of intrinsic enlightenment. At any rate, the Chinese seem to have rejected the Indian position that the enlightenment experience had necessarily to be preceded by a lengthy period—indeed involving many *kalpas*—of moral and intellectual self-purification. Basing themselves on the idea that "one instant of nonconceptual thought is tantamount to being a Buddha," they argued that the person of quick faculties could "see his original face"; i.e., he could have a moment of direct, unmediated experience of events which would be tantamount to having the vision of a Buddha. He could do this even though he had not spent a long preparatory period of eliminating *kleśa*, analyzing dharmic events in *samādhi*, and so on. Thus there was some question of the time element involved in the realization of one's inherent Buddha-nature, but the basis for such an approach was the idea of intrinsic enlightenment. Consequently, the individual has always been a Buddha, and the sudden manifestation of this ability to see things in their *tathatā* nature is nothing more than the manifestation of innate ability. Moral and intellectual self-purification then proceeds *from* this experience, rather than preceding it.

13. *Yuibutsu yobutsu*, in *Zenyaku Shōbōgenzō*, ed. Nakamura Sōichi (Tokyo: Seishin Shobō, 1971), 4:399.

14. According to Dōgen, the life of the Bodhisattva truly begins when he is able to make an utterly sincere vow to emancipate all living beings. This vow seems to be coterminous with *bodhicittotpāda*: "What is called 'arousing the thought of enlightenment' is to make a vow to emancipate all living beings even when one is not yet emancipated oneself. If one arouses this thought, no matter how humble in appearance one is, one is then the guide of all beings" [Okada Gihō, ed., *Shōbōgenzō shisō taikei* (Hōsei Daigaku Shuppan Kyoku, 1965), 6:113]. The person who cannot make this vow is not really a Bodhisattva.

15. Ibid., p. 118.

16. T. 278, pp. 611b ff.

17. "A Brief Commentary on the *Heart of the Sūtra on the Perfection of Wisdom*," T. 1712, p. 553b. "First, one contemplates form as empty and in this way perfects the practice of *śamatha*."

18. Ibid. "When one contemplates emptiness as identical with form, one perfects the practice of *vipaśyanā* [*kuan*]."

19. Ibid.

20. Ananda K. Coomaraswamy, *Elements of Buddhist Iconography*, 2d ed. (New Delhi: M. Manoharial, 1972), p. 12.

Glossary

The following glossary consists of major technical terms used in this book. They consist of Chinese, Sanskrit, and English terms. The purpose of this glossary is to furnish the Chinese character equivalent for each term. I have also included some titles.

annihilationism　斷

Awakening of Faith (in the Mahāyāna). See Ta-ch'eng ch'i hsin lun

birthless　無生

Buddha-nature　佛性

Buddha with the ten bodies　十身佛

cause　因

Cheng wei-shih lun　成唯識論

ch'ung ch'ung wu-chin chu pan chü-tzu　重重無盡主伴具足

condition　緣

conditioned. *See* obedience to conditions

dependent nature　依他性

derivative　末

Dharma-body　法身

dharma-dhātu pratītyasamutpāda　法界緣起

difference　異

different essence　異體

discriminated nature　分別性

disintegration　壞

does not exist in reality　理無

emptiness. *See śūnyatā*

eternalism　常

existence　有

exists to the senses　情有

form　色

function　用

hai in san-mei　海印三昧

hsiang　相
hsing　性
i-ch'eng　一乘
identical essence　同體
identity　同
immutable　不變
includes　入
independent existence. *See svabhāva*
infinite interpenetration　無盡圓融
infinitely repeated possession of retinue by the subject. *See ch'ung ch'ung wu-chin chu pan chü-tzu*
inherent　屬
integration　成
interdependent arising (of the universe). *See dharma-dhātu pratītyasamutpāda*
interpenetration　相入
li　理
limbs. *See derivative*
markless　無相
Mind-only　唯心
mutual identity　相即
mutually causative　相由
mutually creative　相作
nonempty　不空
nonexistence　無
nonexistent in reality　理無
not possessing power　無力
noumenon　理
obedience to conditions　隨緣
One Mind　一心
one vehicle. *See i-ch'eng*
part. *See particularity*
particularity　別
perfect doctrine　圓敎
perfected nature　眞實性
phenomena. *See shih*
possessing power　有力
quasi-existence. *See similar to the real*
result　果
root　本
sāgara-mudrā samādhi. *See hai in san-mei*
samādhi which is like the images of the ocean. *See hai in san-mei*
self-essence. *See svabhāva*

shih 事

shih shih wu-ai 事事無碍

similar to the real 似有

six characteristics 六相

śūnyatā 空

svabhāva 自性

Ta-ch'eng ch'i hsin lun 大乘起信論

T'an hsüan chi 探玄記

tathāgata-garbha 如來藏

things. *See shih*

three natures. *See trisvabhāva*

tradition 宗

trisvabhāva 三性

true emptiness 眞空

universality 總

whole. *See* universality

without an essence 無性

wu-wei 無為

Index